The Map of Meaningful Work
A Practical Guide to Sustaining our Humanity

'An oasis in management literature.'

D.T. Tim Hall, Professor of Organizational
Behavior, Boston University

'When we are lost we become desperate for guidance. Today we are all lost. In this thoughtful volume, the authors give us a precious gift, a map to meaning. It is a gift to be cherished.'

Robert E. Quinn, Author of *Building the Bridge as You Walk on it* and *Deep Change*, Professor of Positive Psychology, Michigan University

'I know from my experience of working with The Map that of all the tools, interventions and frameworks I've used, this is one that consistently adds value to whatever I'm doing. It always works. It always has an impact and engages everybody. It has rigour, there is a strength to the framework, and sufficient space within that for people to construct their own meaning.'

Stephen Tarpey, Human Dimensions, UK

Praise for the previous edition

'I read this book and did all the exercises in it. The book contains an indispensable tool to keep us whole. It will save us from burnout; it will save us from cynicism. It's totally non-judgmental. It's like a key that unlocks all that is important to us as human beings. As a consultant working in developed and developing countries, this framework gives me a simple way to profoundly engage with people across cultures. I can see for the first time not only myself but the context in which I live my life.'

Kerry McGovern, Public Sector Asset, Governance and Financial Management Specialist, K McGovern & Associates, Australia

'Lips-Wiersma and Morris bring the meaning we make of life to a whole new level of understanding in their book. They offer their holistic developmental model as an analytical and practical tool for engaging different pathways of meaning-making in our work and in our lives more generally. The book is overflowing with useful advice and examples of how to engage the model as a means for fostering individual and collective growth, learning and re-becoming whole.'

Jane E. Dutton, Robert L. Kahn University Professor of Business Administration and Psychology, University of Michigan

'I read this book with great delight. It is an important book, as it helps people orientate their career and work–life balance in line with their values and beliefs. It is a rigorous book, thoroughly researched and evidence-based, tried out and tested in various organisational sectors, in different countries and with a range of professions. It is also a dangerous book, as it confronts readers with their inner-most sense of being and challenges them to an intimate conversation with their self.

The human resource professional who wishes to work with human beings, rather than with human resources, will find in this book a useful and easily accessible tool, with numerous illustrations, to help people on their career journeys inside and outside work. It is very well written and deserves a good reception. Highly recommended.'

Yochanan Altman, Senior Professor, Bordeaux School of Management; Research Professor, London Metropolitan University; Visiting Professor, Sorbonne Universities (Pantheon-Assas)

The Map of Meaningful Work

A Practical Guide to Sustaining our Humanity

Second edition

Marjolein Lips-Wiersma
and Lani Morris

Routledge
Taylor & Francis Group

LONDON AND NEW YORK

First published 2011 by Greenleaf as *The Map of Meaning: A Guide to Sustaining our Humanity in the World of Work*

This edition published 2018
by Routledge
2 Park Square, Milton Park, Abingdon, Oxon OX14 4RN

and by Routledge
711 Third Avenue, New York, NY 10017

Routledge is an imprint of the Taylor & Francis Group, an informa business

British Library Cataloguing-in-Publication Data
A catalogue record for this book is available from the British Library

Library of Congress Cataloging-in-Publication Data
A catalog record for this book has been requested

ISBN: 978-1-78353-305-3 (hbk)
ISBN: 978-1-78353-306-0 (pbk)
ISBN: 978-1-351-25206-5 (ebk)

Typeset in Franklin Gothic and Utopia
by Florence Production Ltd, Stoodleigh, Devon

Contents

Dedication and acknowledgements

The search for meaningful work and a meaningful life is so pervasive and energising that we often find ourselves having spontaneous conversations about the topic with people around the world. Virtually every interaction teaches us something about what it is that makes work and life meaningful, and meaningless.

To all those who nurtured our enquiry into meaning: our family and friends; our colleagues; the people who participated in every aspect of our research; those pioneering contributors who courageously tried the work out on themselves and others, as well as in organisations; the authors who have inspired and enriched us; the young students who so easily grasped the essence of meaning; the people who attended workshops and argued with us, and then got inspired to use the Map of Meaning; and all the ordinary people who turn up for work every day, or who work in so many other ways, this book is dedicated to you. We thank and acknowledge you with all our hearts.

1

Introduction and overview

To be human is to search for meaning. Without a sense of meaning, we lose purpose, drive, focus and direction. We notice this when we say, 'I just don't know why I bother: why I bother coming to work, why I bother to live. I just don't see the point'.

Until now we have not had a guide to clearly show what makes work and life meaningful. Now we do.

In this book we introduce you to new knowledge, the **Map of Meaning™**. This gives you a simple, rigorously researched framework, and processes to help you to take charge of the factors that human beings have *agreed* make work and life meaningful. We show you how to increase meaningfulness in your life by harnessing this framework for yourself, whatever your current situation; and how to use it practically to make immediate changes in your organisation, no matter what your position.

Because organisations have such power to influence what happens in the world, it is increasingly important that how they are designed, and who influences this design, is radically rethought. The Map of Meaning is central to this because it provides a practical way to connect the individual to the whole of the organisation, and the whole of the organisation to each individual member, in a meaningful way. It allows us all to participate in the creation of our workplaces.

Human beings want lives and work worthy of their effort and gifts. We want it for ourselves, and we need it collectively. To constantly deny what is most constructive in human beings is to cripple vital talents and energy. Loss of meaning is not just an economic issue, it destroys dignity and destabilises society. Whether in work, looking for work or working in all the ways people do without pay, the longing for meaningful work is both a personal drive, and a socio-political quest.

In the remainder of this chapter we explain why meaningful work is so significant and briefly introduce the research on which the Map of Meaning is based.

In Chapter 2 we break down the rather amorphous term of meaning into workable dimensions, with useful questions for you about meaningful work and life.

Chapters 3, 4 and 5 help you work through the key benefits of having the Map, which are being able to:

- speak powerfully about feelings to do with meaning and its loss;
- make decisions that increase meaningfulness;
- take action to construct a more meaningful life.

In the second part of the book we show how these benefits can be used just as powerfully to transform the world of work.

We conclude by sharing our vision of what having a Map of Meaning can offer our world today, and in the future.

But first, we begin with a brief overview of the context in which meaningful work is gaining so much prominence, and in which our work has so much to offer.

Why meaningful work now?

The quest for meaningful work is not new. Over the centuries there have been many different ways of thinking about the meaning of work, many of which have to some degree, influenced the design of the contemporary workplace. From Marx, Weber and Hawthorne: work as alienation, as salvation, and intrinsic motivation at work, through to modern concerns about employee engagement and human flourishing, ideas influence how we think about work. However, these currently emerge against a background of increasing disengagement, disempowerment and an ever-accelerating pace of work and life, all expressions of meaninglessness.

The interest in the purpose and practice of work is also driven by recent research showing that meaningful work has a significant impact on work outcomes. Numerous studies show conclusively that meaningful work, or its absence, influences outcomes in organisational life such as: work motivation, absenteeism, work behaviour, engagement, job satisfaction, empowerment, stress, performance and personal well-being (Rosso *et al.* 2010).

However, the quest for meaningful work is much more than an individualised quest for self-realisation, or an organisational quest for employee engagement. It is a socio-political project, concerned with sustaining and enriching our humanity and therefore our capacity to respond to the local and global challenges which face us and the planet. Because the world's direction and future are created through organisations, be they commercial, community, not for profit, local or global, how we design organisations is vital. It shapes who we become as human beings, inside and outside of work; and who we are and what we do in organisations shapes our individual and collective future.

To redesign work requires the courage and humility to question fundamental ways of thinking about organising, and about who decides how we organise. To lift the human quest for meaningful work to the strategic level, where it can influence our thinking and the design of organisations, we must:

- claim the language that enables us to speak about meaning;

- work from a constructive view of humanity in which we acknowledge that the drive for meaning is a profound human motivation;

- ensure that every human being knows what is and is not meaningful and therefore needs to be part of how the workplace and society are constructed.

In the following section we show how the Map of Meaning offers us a practical way to recreate work and organisations.

Finding the language to speak about what matters most

The words we use create and shape our reality. Thus, to make meaningfulness an ongoing part of the way we work, it is essential to find and claim the language that enables us to speak about meaning. This helps us raise human concerns in the day-to-day experience of work amidst a language of effectiveness, efficiency and accountability. It is only when the language of meaning is claimed, and used, that it can impact organisational decision making, strategy, culture, structure and purpose.

Words direct our attention, get translated in practices and priorities and ultimately reproduce what is and is not legitimate to talk about in organisations. For example, categorising management into 'soft' and 'hard' is not just an innocent labelling of management practices. The '*hard*' is interpreted as the *management* that makes plans, sets up structures and monitors performance. The '*soft*' is concerned with day-to-day experience and motivation of employees. In using words that separate these and that are not neutral (who wants to be soft?), a common currency is created. Some currencies (hard) are valued higher than others (soft). The 'hard' dominates, yet the 'soft' determines who, collectively, we become as human beings. Do we become more skilled, more energised and proactive, more thoughtful and better equipped as citizens? Or do we become disheartened, hardened, cynical and alienated from ourselves and others? We do not assert that reclaiming meaningful conversations will, alone, change long-established organisational patterns. We do argue and show that using the Map of Meaning can legitimise and enable meaningful conversations involving everyone in the organisation. This is at the very foundation of creating fundamental and lasting change.

Claiming our constructive Self

Talking about meaning is, in itself, not enough to reclaim our human concerns at work. While we found that people talk about meaning every day, most of these conversations are negative, focusing on the absence of meaning; for example – 'what is the point of this?' (policy, practice, change initiative). As a result, conversations about meaning tend to reinforce people's experience of themselves as powerless, which increases meaninglessness. The Map of Meaning provides a way for people to claim their positive longing to do work worthy of their talents and energy.

There are many obstacles to meaningful work, and removing them is no mean feat. Precisely because of this, it is important that each individual in an organisation works from a place of strength and dignity. Each person needs to be able to recognise that when they say, 'I don't see the point of this', they are not complaining but articulating their frustrated need for meaning. In the same way that our body is not satisfied by just recognising that we need to eat; our hunger for meaning requires action. Recognising this, we can change conversations of passive lament into conversations of hope and energy.

Every employee in the organisation knows what is meaningful

Once we have constructive language, recognising where work is meaningful, where more meaning needs to be created, and where current meaning is in danger of being destroyed, we need to take action. At present, the values-based discussion in organisations (where it takes place at all) is almost entirely claimed by the focus on 'leadership', and where positive change is called for, we increasingly call for 'more leadership'. Yet, recent research shows that no employee spontaneously mentions leadership when talking about meaningful work (Bailey and Madden 2016).

In contrast, the fundamental reality that this book claims is that everybody in the organisation knows what is, and is not, meaningful. Reclaiming meaning is a bottom-up task which needs to be facilitated, but not directed, by those who have formal power in organisations.

Since power corresponds with the human ability not just to act but to act together (Hannah Arendt), we need a collective discourse that answers the questions:

- What really matters to us as human beings?

- What do we and the organisations in which we work need to do to remove obstacles to meaningful work?

- How do we create opportunities to have more meaningful work?

These questions position the quest for meaningful work in the socio-political realm and remind us that we are the designers and creators of the organisations in which we work.

The economist and philosopher E. F. Schumacher (1978: 14) noted that without a map of what we 'really care about', human beings 'hesitate, doubt, change their minds, run hither and thither, uncertain not simply of how to get what they want, but above all of what they want'. At present this seems to be a prevailing pattern in organisations. Change is inevitable, but often results in contradictory practices, the removal of practices that employees really care about, and increasing layers of complexity that disconnect individuals at all levels of the organisation from the end result of their work. The Map of Meaning helps us design organisations in ways that support the human need for meaning. Working with it leads to a simple and integrative way of assessing organisational practices and taking action. When we work with it, people say 'I now know what really matters to me and to others. I know what needs to be done next'.

The Map of Meaning is research based

Like all reliable maps, the Map of Meaning has been carefully tested. It is based on over 17 years' research into the insights and practice of ordinary people, published in high-quality, peer-reviewed academic journals.

The Map of Meaning was developed by Marjolein Lips-Wiersma, based on an in-depth collaborative process that answers the question of 'when do I find my work meaningful?' The research found that people have meaning in their work when they experience: 'expressing full potential'; 'unity with others'; 'serving others' and 'integrity with self' (referred to as 'developing the inner self' in the research) (Lips-Wiersma 2002; Lips-Wiersma and Wright 2012a, b).

This research showed that:

- Meaning is not so personal and subjective that it cannot be worked with in organisations.

- People have *common* experiences of what creates and diminishes meaningful work. As a result, most organisational practices that create meaningful work are applicable to all employees.

- Work is experienced in very similar ways across cultures. The words might be different. For example, an American person might really like 'inspiration', whereas while working in Japan, we found the Japanese preferred 'hope'. Both cultures felt that articulating a vision of possible, positive futures was one part of what made work meaningful.

Further research (Lips-Wiersma, Soutter and Wright 2015) appears to confirm and also enhance many of the positive psychology findings, by showing that meaning creation requires a process, not just a desire to live meaningfully.

A further paper, (Lips-Wiersma, Wright and Dik 2016), highlights that it is not just privileged workers who search for meaningfulness in their work. Blue- and pink-collar workers also place enormous importance on meaning, although, not surprisingly, they experience less of certain meanings, particularly 'expressing full potential'.

In 2017 a paper was published on how the different dimensions of meaningful work (unity with others, expressing full potential, integrity with self, and service to others) relate to each other. This shows that meaning is not a simple list of things to articulate or experience, but that it is an ongoing process of discovering and creating balance between the dimensions of meaning, so that, for example, 'serving others' is not expressed at the exclusion of 'unity with others' or 'integrity with self'.

The Map captures these findings in a simple, profound and practical diagram that makes understanding and working with the key issues of meaning clear and accessible to everyone. All these findings are continually tested in practice in the field.

So *how* does the Map help and the book work?

In this book we often talk about meaningful work and life. While the research was done on work and organisations, it is in the very nature of meaningfulness that it speaks to the whole person across a number of life-roles, including work. What we learn and experience at work transfers to other roles and vice versa. Together with numerous practitioners (managers, teachers, consultants, community coordinators, CEOs and employees), we have identified ten guiding principles that are central to creating and sustaining meaningful life and work. These form the foundation of the structure of this book.

1 **To create meaningful work we need a map that makes it easy to work with meaning.**
   The Map of Meaning is a clear, simple framework, easily grasped and easily used in a variety of ways. It makes the dimensions and process of meaningfulness clear and easily understood (Chapter 2).

2 **To work with meaning we need to be able to first identify it for ourselves, and next speak about it confidently with others.**
   We show how the Map helps you speak about what matters most to you, speak to others about this in ways that make our differences

and commonalities visible, and then move to constructive action (Chapter 3).

3 **Meaning gets lost when we are out of balance for too long.**
We show how the Map helps us see and address fundamental tensions between the needs of Self and those of Others, as well as our need to both Be and Do, and constantly reassess these in our work and life (Chapter 4).

4 **A meaningful life is whole and increasingly coherent.**
We show how the Map of Meaning helps you bring fragmented life and work experiences together into an increasingly integrated whole (Chapter 4).

5 **A meaningful life is a responsible life and we need to be able to stay in charge of what makes life meaningful for us.**
In Chapter 5 we show how the Map of Meaning helps us take responsibility for increasing meaningfulness for ourselves, and learning to co-create it with others.

6 **For life and work to be meaningful we need to be both inspired and grounded in reality.**
We show how the Map of Meaning helps us stay in touch with our sources of inspiration while staying fully connected to the reality of ourselves (including our imperfections), and our circumstances (such as the conditions in which we work and the economic conditions in which our work takes place) (Chapter 5).

7 **For life and work to be meaningful we need to be able to have conversations about what future; immediate or distant, local or global, we *do* want to create.**
Attending to what is meaningful engages and strengthens human dignity and power, enabling a constructive engagement with future challenges (Chapter 5).

8 **Work can be far more meaningful if organisational conversations, practices and purposes support the human need for meaning.**
If meaningful work is ignored, made invisible or in some way seen as inferior to an ideal of the organisation as an efficient machine, meaning is easily lost. Through a variety of case studies, we show how when meaningful work becomes a foundational principle of organising it leads to responsible, realistic, whole-systems practices and structures in organisations (Chapters 6, 7 and 8).

9   **The responsibility revolution requires us to redefine the very nature of work and the purposes to which it is put.**

In Chapter 9 we show how the dimensions of personal meaning are naturally in complete synergy with social and environmental responsibility. The Map therefore helps us create internal and external systems that are integrated and have integrity built into every aspect of organising.

10   **Meaningfulness is more easily achieved with others who are concerned with the same aim.**

We look forward to a growing, interactive community of workers, practitioners, leaders, trainers and consultants who work with the Map. In Appendix 1 we outline how you can work with us and how we can work with you.

From the feedback we have had so far, people prefer to read the book in different ways. Some choose to do the exercises first as they understand best through experiential learning. Others want to first obtain a practical or intellectual understanding and read the book before they do the exercises. Yet others are interested in particular segments of the book such as 'wholeness' or 'taking charge' and start reading there before finding out how these topics connect to all the others in the book. We invite you to read and work with the book in the way that best suits you. Most of all, we invite you to find out for yourself what difference working with the Map of Meaning can make for you, because it only comes alive when you use it for yourself and begin to take control of creating more meaningful work and living a more meaningful and satisfying life.

To begin with, in the next chapter we will introduce you to the Map that forms the heart of our work.

2

Background and guide to the Map of Meaning

In this chapter we introduce you to the Map of Meaning. We do this in some detail so that you clearly understand the elements of the map before applying it, as we do, in various contexts in the following chapters.

Opening up the black box of meaning

When, in academic research, employees score high on items such as 'my work is meaningful' or 'my work is worthwhile', they also report increasing health and well-being, and employees who have meaningful work are more loyal, committed and creative. However, what it means to have meaningful work has not been deeply researched. It is usually assumed that meaningful work is work that 'makes a difference'. Our findings showed that the construct of meaning is so much richer than that. This is important because only when we open the complex box of meaning, and understand all aspects of the way humans construct it, can we start to individually and collectively create more of it.

Figure 2.1 shows the prerequisites for meaningful work, and the outcomes that come from meaningful work as shown by research. The centre, the factors that together make up what human beings agree makes work meaningful,

Figure 2.1

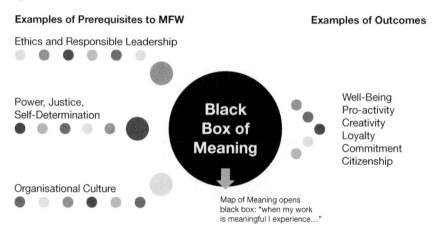

has to this point remained unexplored. Thus organisations have tried to work with what has essentially been a black box. Our work enables us to open up, understand and work with this area of human experience.

In the remainder of this chapter we open up this box and introducing the key dimensions that make up the framework of the Map of Meaning (Figure 2.2), using many of the words of our research participants so you can see how it was built up from real-life experience. You may recognise many of your own experiences in their words. We include the key questions that can help you answer 'what makes work meaningful to me'?

The seven dimensions of the map

There are three main aspects to the map.

The first is the **four pathways to meaningful work**; this shows us that human beings find meaning through the fulfilment of these four aspects of their lives. These are: **Integrity with Self, Unity with Others, Service to Others** and **Expressing Full Potential**.

Second, these four pathways are held in two **tensions** between apparently opposing desires, the drive to meet the needs of the **Self** and the need to meet the needs of **Others**; and the need for **Being** (reflection) as well as the need for **Doing** (action).

Third, all these elements are played out in the overall context of **Inspiration** and the **Reality of our Self and our Circumstances**.

We will cover each aspect of the map in the following sections.

Figure 2.2 **The Map of Meaning**™

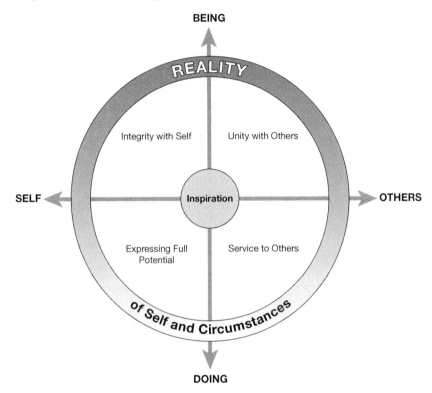

The four pathways to meaningful work and meaningful living

In this section we give clear descriptions of the four main pathways that are the foundation of meaningful work and meaningful living. We describe each pathway as a whole, then describe the sub-themes that make it up, with:

- a general description;

- a variety of words and stories used by the research participants;

- quotes to show that human beings have always been engaged with this aspect of meaningfulness;

- questions to ask ourselves and our organisations to better access meaning in ourselves or have conversations with others at the most accessible level.

Integrity with Self

This dimension of meaningful work points to the meaningfulness that arises as we question the person we are becoming as a result of being engaged in our life and work. Do we become a kinder, more self-aware person, or the opposite? Depending on one's world-view, Integrity with Self can be based on simply wanting to be a good person. Or, it can mean developing the self that God wants us to be, or becoming the higher self within us. Or, it can be some combination of all these. At the heart of this pathway is the idea that an unexamined life is not worth living, and who we become as a result of being engaged in work, and in other parts of our lives, greatly matters to us as human beings. Sometimes this is harder for us to see, but our family and friends may easily recognise the effect our work is having on us.

People in workshops spoke about this pathway in the following ways:

- to stay close to myself;

- being a good person;

- being comfortable in my skin;

- be the change you want to see in the world;

- I strive for love and harmony within my inner self;

- courage/boldness of being who we are meant to be;

- saying yes to the voice of God within me.

We found that within the need to develop and become ourselves, there are three main sub-themes: **moral development**, **personal growth** and **being true to self**. Self-awareness is embedded in all three sub-themes.

Moral development

This aspect of Integrity with Self highlights the moral nature of our character and the ability to make a distinction between right and wrong.

People in workshops spoke about moral development in the following ways:

- honesty;

- trustworthiness;

- discerning the effects of my actions and interactions on others;

- developing character;

- being a good person;

- having the courage to do what is right rather than convenient;

- not compromising myself (too much).

An example of how people experienced this at work is: 'Currently we have many discussions about "what is the right thing to do here"'.

Many well-known sayings reinforce the universality and enduring relevance of this theme for human beings:

> The sad truth is that most evil is done by people who never make up their minds to be either good or evil.
>
> Hannah Arendt

> Great necessities call out great virtues.
>
> Abigail Adams

> I know only that what is moral is what you feel good after and what is immoral is what you feel bad after.
>
> Ernest Hemingway

> Two things awe me most, the starry sky above me and the moral law within me.
>
> Immanuel Kant

> We do not act rightly because we have virtue or excellence, but we rather have those because we have acted rightly.
>
> Aristotle

> Easy to do are things that are bad and not beneficial to oneself, but very, very difficult indeed to do is that which is beneficial and good.
>
> Buddhism, Dhammapada: 163

In order to think about how this aspect of meaning is playing out in our work/life, it can be useful to ask ourselves such questions as:

- When do I ask myself, What is the right thing to do? In what situations do I forget to ask this question?

- When did I last think about the right thing to do in a situation? When did I do the right thing? Why did I make this choice?

- How does what I think is 'right' relate to what others might think is 'right'—at work? in other areas of my life?

- Have I felt upset by the ethical implications of decisions made at work?

- What in my work encourages, or discourages, me to do the right thing?

- What are the conditions in organisations that support or damage moral development?

- How can we create an environment where we notice and can discuss what is right to do?

Personal growth

This covers both the idea of growth as deliberately 'cultivated', and of allowing growth to come naturally into existence.

People in workshops spoke about personal growth in the following ways:

- expanding;

- revealing insights and new ways;

- developing my strengths and accepting my limitations;

- awareness of skill and knowledge gaps and addressing these;

- continuous learning;

- being ready to fulfil my role to the best of my ability;

- being responsible for my talents.

An example of how people experienced this at work is: 'With new responsibilities parts of myself emerged that I did not know I had. I was blossoming'.

Many sayings reinforce the universality and enduring relevance of this theme for human beings:

> You must learn day by day, year by year, to broaden your horizon. The more things you love, the more you are interested in, the more you enjoy, the more you are indignant about, the more you have left when anything happens.
>
> Ethel Barrymore

> To be what we are, and to become what we are capable of becoming, is the only end of life.
>
> Robert Louis Stevenson

Of all the things that can have an effect on your future, I believe personal growth is the greatest. We can talk about sales growth, profit growth, asset growth, but all of this probably will not happen without personal growth.

Jim Rohn

Doest thou believe thyself to be a puny form, when the universe is folded within thee?

Baha'u'llah

The Master said, 'At fifteen I set my heart upon learning. At thirty, I had planted my feet upon firm ground. At forty, I no longer suffered from perplexities. At fifty, I knew what the biddings of heaven were. At sixty, I heard them with a docile ear. At seventy, I could follow the dictates of my own heart; for what I desired no longer overstepped the boundaries of right'.

Analects of Confucius, 2: 4

In order to think about how this aspect of meaning is playing out in our work and life, it can be useful to ask ourselves such questions as:

- If someone asked, can I come up with examples of how I have grown as a result of being engaged in this work?

- Am I becoming more or less ready to fulfil my role to the best of my ability?

- Am I still learning or am I standing still? If the latter, is that a conscious choice?

- What are the conditions in my organisation that stimulate, and stifle, personal growth?

Being true to self

This focuses on the aspects of not being false, being in accordance with the reality of oneself and being in perfect tune with one's self.

People in workshops spoke about being true to self in the following ways:

- the freedom to be me;

- being able to question;

- authenticity;

- sticking to my own priorities;

- uniqueness;

- respect;

- self-worth;

- knowing my own mind.

An example of how people experienced this at work is: 'I can be me in this organisation. I can dress in feminine clothes, be serious, be light, be me'.

Sayings that reinforce the universality and enduring relevance of this theme for human beings:

> Before his death Rabbi Zusya said 'In the coming world, they will not ask me "why were you not Moses?" They will ask me "Why were you not Zusya?"'
>
> Hasidic story

> At bottom every man knows well enough that he is a unique being, only once on this earth; and by no extraordinary chance will such a marvellously picturesque piece of diversity in unity as he is, ever be put together a second time.
>
> Friedrich Nietzsche

> Just being yourself, being who you are, is a successful rebellion.
>
> Author unknown

> You might as well be yourself, everyone else is taken.
>
> Attributed to Oscar Wilde

To check out this aspect of Integrity with Self you can ask:

- Am I becoming more or less myself as a result of being engaged in this work?

- When do I wear a mask? Why?

- When am I fully me? What are the consequences of being fully me, compared with being masked?

- What are the organisational conditions that call out our true self and which ones alienate us from our self?

Unity with Others

This pathway refers to the meaningfulness of living together with other human beings. Unity does not mean uniformity. It requires a balancing with 'expressing full potential' to not only be in unity with others but also express our unique talents and identity.

At the heart of this pathway is understanding that humanity is essentially one and that experiencing this is what enriches our humanity.

People in workshops put the following words to this pathway:

- being with my mates;

- it's all about teamwork;

- we can do more together than alone;

- being part of a community;

- we are all one, the interconnectedness of it all;

- I am because you are;

- living in and with and through each other, lives woven in love with each other;

- synergy is the result of more than one person pooling energy;

- iron sharpens iron—deep calls to deep. Maturity comes through interaction;

- see God in each other;

- in my experience our hearts connect when we talk about our deeper values, even though we might not agree.

Within the pathway of Unity with Others, we found three main sub-themes. These are: **working together**, **shared values** and **belonging**. Relatedness is embedded in all three sub-themes.

Working together

This sub-theme points to the sense that we can be more and achieve more with the support of others.

People in workshops spoke about working together in the following ways:

- stimulation from others;

- overcoming shared obstacles;

- team;

- fun;

- mutually motivating;

- energy;

- feeling 'in kilter' with others brings validity to one's own work;

- cooperation.

An example of how people experienced this at work is: 'I probably would not have got into this line of work had my father not been involved in it. But Dad and I got on really well together, and I shared his enthusiasm for the business and the plans we had for expansion and it just flowed naturally from there'.

Sayings that reinforce the universality and enduring relevance of this theme for human beings:

> We must learn to live together as brothers or perish together as fools.
>
> Martin Luther King Jr

> As long as you keep a person down, some part of you has to be down there to hold him down, so it means you cannot soar as you other-wise might.
>
> Marian Anderson

> All is rooted in reciprocity.
>
> Sri Yukteswar

> Individually, we are one drop. Together, we are an ocean.
>
> Ryunosuke Satoro

> Every kingdom divided against itself is laid waste, and no city or house divided against itself will stand.
>
> Matthew 12: 25

And, again, we can check on how this aspect of meaning is in our lives by asking:

- Do I work with, or against, other people?

- Do I enjoy working with my colleagues?

- Do I experience mutual support in my relationships at work?

- What do I do that encourages collegiality, and what might I sometimes do that might make that more difficult?

- What makes it easier for people to work well with each other in my organisation? What gets in the way of people working well together?

Sharing values

This covers the concepts of articulating values, making values public and having values in common.

People in workshops spoke about sharing values in the following ways:

- making our assumptions visible;

- shared conversations about values;

- not having to justify things as there is a common understanding of our values;

- sharing our knowing and our not knowing;

- talking about why we do what we do before we actually go and do things;

- making deeper conversation possible.

An example of how people experienced this at work is: 'I need to find some sort of bond with people, some common shared beliefs or value that you place on humanity in the broader sense of the word. And I get quite excited when I locate people like that at work because you don't come across them too often'.

A saying that reinforces the universality and enduring relevance of this theme in being human:

> First we talked about our purposes, then we agreed.
> Mayan saying

> Without commonly shared and widely entrenched moral values and obligations, neither the law, not democratic government, nor even the market economy will function properly.
> Vaclav Havel

> Grief can take care of itself, but to get the full value of joy you must have somebody to share it with.
> Mark Twain

The power of a movement lies in the fact that it can indeed change the habits of people. This change is not the result of force but of dedication, of moral persuasion.

Stephen Biko

Set your expectations high; find men and women whose integrity and values you respect; get their agreement on a course of action; and give them your ultimate trust.

John Fellows Akers

The first step in the evolution of ethics is a sense of solidarity with other human beings.

Albert Schweitzer

If you want to see how much you feel you share values with others, these questions might help:

- How often do we talk at work about why we do what we do?

- In my work, can I talk about what deeply matters to me? Can others?

- Do I sometimes choose to hide my values?

- What conditions at work help us to ask, Why are we doing this? What happens when we do? What are the underlying values and assumptions in our decision making?

Belonging

In this we see highlighted the idea of being a member of, connected with, and classed among a group, which points to the human need to be a part of a larger association with whom we feel deeply at home.

People in workshops spoke about belonging in the following ways:

- generosity;

- warmth;

- being part of;

- being at home among;

- acceptance;

- not having to justify;

- celebrating together;

- feeling embraced;

- community.

An example of how people experienced this at work is:

> There are times when I look around at the people I work with and think how lucky I am to be part of this group, these people with such passion for the theatre, all these young people that are so dedicated, and the teachers who are so committed to the difference theatre can make. I pinch myself. It's like coming home.

Two of the many quotes that reinforce the universality and enduring relevance of this theme are from John O'Donohue:

> No soul/individual is sealed off or hermetically self-enclosed. Although each soul is individual and unique, by its very nature the soul hungers for relationship. Consequently, it is your soul that longs to belong—and it is your soul that makes all belonging possible.
>
> 2000: 17

> The hunger to belong is not merely a desire to be attached to something. It is rather sensing that great transformation and discovery become possible when belonging is sheltered and true.
>
> 1998: 22

Normally we know if we don't feel a sense of belonging, but if you want to think about it more directly you can ask yourself:

- Do I experience high-quality/deep connections with other people at work?

- Do I feel 'out of place' at work?

- Do I feel a sense of companionship at work?

- What encourages people at work? Do people feel part of a community? When do they feel alone?

Expressing full potential

This pathway refers to the meaningfulness of sounding our own note in the universe. It is different from Integrity with Self because it is active and outward directed, whereas the former is inward and reflective. At the heart of this pathway are the concepts that we are all unique, and that we are responsible for bringing our unique gifts and talents into the world.

The following quote from Marianne Williamson's book *A Return to Love*, and often erroneously attributed to Nelson Mandela, is as popular as it is because it so clearly captures both our longing and our anxiousness about expressing our full potential:

> Our deepest fear is not that we are inadequate. Our deepest fear is that we are powerful beyond measure. It is our light, not our darkness, that most frightens us. We ask ourselves, who am I to be brilliant, gorgeous, talented and fabulous? Actually, who are you not to be? You are a child of God. Your playing small doesn't serve the world. There is nothing enlightened about shrinking so that other people won't feel insecure around you. We are born to make manifest the glory of God that is within us. It is not just in some of us; it is in everyone. And as we let our own light shine, we unconsciously give other people permission to do the same. As we are liberated from our fears, our presence automatically liberates others.
>
> Williamson 1992

People in workshops spoke about this pathway in the following ways:

- doing my best work at all times;

- being responsible for making the most use of my gifts and talents;

- the delight in knowing that I've done a good piece of work;

- find out what you are good at and do more of it!;

- freedom to express;

- having a good idea heard and acted on;

- individuality in all its forms;

- soulful writing, dancing, working;

- every act is an act of will and therefore creative—conscious living;

- sounding my note in the universe.

Generally, we found that Expressing Full Potential could be found in three main sub-themes. These are **creating**, **achieving** and **influencing**.

Creating

This covers the need to bring into existence, give rise to or originate.

People in workshops spoke about creating in the following ways:

- enjoyment of making things;

- love of exploration and expression;

- having an outlet to express me;

- creative flow;

- energy towards a vision;

- adding my bits to the bigger picture;

- beauty;

- freedom to take a project where I want to take it.

An example of this in the workplace is:

> I pour my energy now into my oyster farm and that to me is social and economic development for the community. And the oyster farm is to me like my painting. I'm creating something in the area where oyster farming was always deemed unviable; we just decided we would make it work.

Many sayings reinforce the universality and enduring relevance of this theme for human beings:

> A bird doesn't sing because it has an answer, it sings because it has a song.
> Maya Angelou

> Sometimes creativity just means the daily work of helping others to see a problem in a different way.
> Joseph Badaracco

> There is a vitality, a life force, an energy, a quickening, which is translated through you into action. And because there is only one you in all time, this expression is unique and if you block it, it will never exist through any other medium and the world will not have it.
> Martha Graham in a letter to Agnes de Mille

Though organisations and individuals know that creativity is valuable, it is useful sometimes to check on how much of it we are able to experience:

- Do I have times when I am so engaged with my work that I lose track of time?

- How much can I really apply my gifts and talents at work?

- Am I stimulated to be creative at work or discover new ways of doing things at work?

- Can I apply my new ideas or concepts at work?

- Do I get excited or enthusiastic about what we create?

- What encourages people to feel creative at my workplace?

- What stops people from contributing to their unique gifts and talents?

Achieving

In this sub-theme we acknowledge the human need to accomplish, to carry things out to their conclusion.

People in workshops spoke about achieving in the following ways:

- benchmarking;

- just do it;

- the meaning that comes from mastering something;

- ambition;

- recognition;

- success;

- completing a piece of work;

- competent;

- effective;

- improving standards.

A work example of this is: 'There is an inherent meaning in mastering something. When something comes out of my hands that I know to be good, it is a great feeling'.

Many sayings reinforce the universality and enduring relevance of this theme for human beings:

> My grandfather once told me that there were two kinds of people: those who do the work and those who take the credit. He told me to try to be in the first group; there was much less competition.
>
> Indira Gandhi

When you practise excellence you are not trying to be better than anyone else. You are trying to be the best you can be.

Linda Kavelin Popov

Whoever I am and whatever I am doing, some kind excellence is within my reach.

John W. Gardner

Achievement seems to be connected with action. Successful men and women keep moving. They make mistakes, but they don't quit.

Conrad Hilton

Questions you may want to ask yourself to get a sense of how much you feel you are achieving:

- Do I regularly experience a sense of achievement?

- Where and when is this not happening? What stops me?

- What do I long to achieve? What would be the first step to doing this?

- How often do individuals in my organisation have a sense of achievement?

- How often do they have a sense of failure? What causes these differing experiences?

Influencing

Influencing covers our need to affect destiny, or have in some way the power to bring something about.

People in workshops spoke about influencing in the following ways:

- getting others on board;

- inspiring others;

- reminding others of why we do what we do;

- improving conditions for those less powerful;

- offering direction;

- drawing attention to important issues;

- setting an example.

Examples of how people experienced this at work are: 'In this role I can actively help shape the organisation', and in this story where someone was able to take a small action and solve a problem, 'We had a problem with the manager. But I went to see him and we got our trolleys back'.

A wonderful story that captures the creativity with which an individual can choose to influence is in Werner Herzog's autobiography.

> In 1974 we German filmmakers were still fragile, and when a friend told me Lotte [Eisner] had suffered a massive stroke and I should get on the next plane to Paris, I made the decision not to fly. It was not the right thing to do, and because I just could not accept that she might die, I walked from Munich to her apartment in Paris. I put on a shirt, grabbed a bundle of clothes, a map and a compass and set off in a straight line, sleeping under bridges, in farms and abandoned houses . . . I walked against her death, knowing that if I walked on foot she would be alive when I got there. And that is just what happened. Lotte lived until the age of ninety or there-abouts, and years after the walk, and she was nearly blind etc., she said to me, 'Werner there is still this spell cast over me that I am not allowed to die. I am tired of life. It would be a good time for me now.' Joking I said, 'OK Lotte, I hereby take the spell away.' Three weeks later she died.
>
> Herzog and Cronin 2002: 281

To test our sense of being able to influence we can ask:

- What can I influence?

- How much am I able to influence?

- What would I like to influence more? What could enable me to do so?

- What are the conditions at work under which every individual can have a say in the things that affect them?

Service to Others

Serving others is about the human need to make a contribution to the well-being of others, from helping an individual to making a difference in the wider world.

People in workshops spoke about this pathway in the following ways:

- if you help one, you help all;

- good people help others;

- if you think you are too small to make a difference, try sleeping in a closed room with a mosquito;

- to give and not to count the costs;

- unconditional love;

- generosity of spirit;

- by serving others you come closer to self-realisation, acceptance and ultimately peace;

- love thy neighbour as thyself;

- how can I act in this moment in a way that uplifts me and others?

- I'm here for something bigger than myself;

- what is the point of my life if it is only for me?

Within the overall human need to serve others we found two sub-themes. They are: **making a difference** and **meeting the needs of humanity and the planet**.

Making a difference

This sub-theme covers being able to improve things for others and can cover helping to improve people's experience of things, or assisting them to improve their conditions.

People in workshops spoke about making a difference in the following ways:

- giving back;

- advocating for the needs of others;

- helping others grow;

- supporting colleagues in hard times;

- challenging ideas that do not benefit employees;

- speaking up.

Examples of how people experienced this at work are: 'I know that the organisation is ever so slightly better off because I'm here'; 'I'm aware now that we provide work for a certain amount of people. To me that's very important'; and 'I used to feel that I could really assist our clients, now I no longer have time for that'.

Many sayings reinforce the universality and enduring relevance of this theme for human beings:

> We don't set out to save the world; we set out to wonder how other people are doing and to reflect on how our actions affect other people's hearts.
>
> Pema Chödrön

> We must not, in trying to think about how we can make a big difference, ignore the small daily difference we can make which, over time, add up to big differences that we often cannot foresee.
>
> Marian Wright Edelman

> Caring can be learned by all human beings, can be worked into the design of every life, meeting an individual need as well as a pervasive need in society.
>
> Mary Catherine Bateson

> Bad things happen because good people stand by and do nothing.
>
> Edmund Burke – paraphrased

> Work if performed in the spirit of service is worship.
>
> Baha'u'llah

And if we want to check out this aspect of meaningful work we can ask:

- Do I help others in my workplace?

- Do I feel that what I do makes a real difference?

- Are employees given the time and freedom to make a difference?

- Does the work we do make a difference to others?

- Do I allow others the opportunity to help and support me?

- When does the work I do most directly contribute to others? How can I increase this?

Meeting the needs of humanity and the planet

This points to the need to be useful in the larger context, to feel that one's life and work have been useful to a wider cause, that it helps to meet the needs of wider groups, of the wider world, or of the planet itself. It differs from making a difference, where research participants referred to the elements of their work over which they had more immediate control and which were internal to the organisation.

People in workshops spoke about meeting the needs of humanity and the planet in the following ways:

- social action;

- helping the poor and the unemployed;

- sharing resources;

- acting with future generations in mind;

- having a universal consciousness;

- giving back;

- empowering the community.

Examples of how people experienced this at work are: 'I work for a company that does good work'; 'We've just done this massive "vision thing" but our company makes no real contribution to human well-being'; 'Will it all be worthwhile if we destroy the planet as a result of our growth?'

Many sayings reinforce the universality and enduring relevance of this theme for human beings:

> For the sake of the welfare of all, carry on thy task in life.
>
> Bhagavad Gita 3: 20

> One thing I know: the only ones among you who will really be happy are those who will have sought and found how to serve.
>
> Albert Schweitzer

> How wonderful it is that nobody need wait a single moment before starting to improve the world.
>
> Anne Frank

> Act as if what you do makes a difference. It does.
>
> William James

In the following words from Olive Schreiner we hear the longing to leave an enduring legacy to future generations so hauntingly expressed.

> I would like to say to the men and women of the generations which will come after us. 'You will look back at us with astonishment. You

> will wonder at the passionate struggles that accomplished so little.
> . . . at the truths we grasped at, but never could quite get our fingers
> round—but, what you will never know is how it was thinking of you
> and for you, that we struggled as we did . . . that it was in the
> thought of your larger realisation and fuller life that we found
> consolation for the futilities of our own'.
>
> Olive Schreiner, *Women and Labour* 1911

We can hope that our work is a contribution, but if you want to question how much your work contributes to the whole, you might ask yourself:

- Do I contribute to products or services that enhance human well-being?

- Do we take the environment into consideration in all aspects of our work?

- Do we do work that matters or is worthwhile?

- Does the organisation really stand for something that matters or is worthwhile, or is it all lip-service?

Tensions between Doing and Being and between Self and Others

We have just covered, in detail, the four dimensions of meaningful work. However, meeting the needs of each pathway sets up **tensions**. Too much focus on one can lead to an overall loss of meaning. For example, if we are overly focused on expressing full potential, we might lose connections with others, or if we are overly focused on serving others, we might lose ourselves. The important point here is not that our working lives always have to be perfectly balanced, but that, because all four dimensions activate the experience of meaningful work, missing out on one of them, over time, creates loss of meaning. Another important point is that the different dimensions strengthen each other. For example, research has shown that those who have good relationships at work (unity) also exhibit more prosocial behaviour (service to others), and that those better understand and develop their own unique talents (expressing full potential) are also better able to help others. It is therefore important to create work in which people can experience all pathways to meaningful work, and it is important for individuals as well as organisations to identify where this is not the case, and address the loss.

Meaning is found in working through *all* pathways, and in how we balance or address fundamental tensions. In our research we found two **tensions that lie at the heart of meaning**: one between **Being** and **Doing**, and the next between **Self** and **Others**. Because, to some extent, these are always in tension with each other, imbalance easily occurs so it is important to be able to map the extent to which each dimension is experienced at work.

Being and Doing

Being and Doing highlights the need to both focus inward and reflect, and to act in the world.

Being focuses on the need to ponder. It covers such things as silence, patience, taking our time, checking in with our bodies or thoughtful togetherness. We can be not only with one's self but also with others.

This is a universal and enduring theme:

> What is this life if, full of care, / We have no time to stand and stare?
> W.H. Davies, 'Leisure'

> And when is there time to remember, to sift, to weigh, to estimate, to total?
> Tillie Olsen

> It is being that speaks within us and not we who speak of being.
> Merleau-Ponty

Doing is about action; it focuses out into the world. It is heard when we catch ourselves or others saying: 'I just can't wait to get my hands on that clay' or 'We've talked enough, let's get on with it' or 'I just want to get started right now'.

The need to act is a universal and enduring theme too:

> What would life be if we had no courage to attempt anything?
> Vincent van Gogh

> Do you want to know who you are? Don't ask. Act! Action will delineate and define you.
> Thomas Jefferson

And if we want to check out this aspect of meaningful work and living we can ask:

- At work, do I often feel overwhelmed by the amount I have to do?

- In my work do I have the time and space to think? What is the effect of this on me and on my work?

- Would we make better decisions at work if we took more time to be thoughtful and reflect on what we are doing and why?

- At work do we have a good balance between focusing on getting things done and noticing how people are feeling?

Self and Others

The tension between Self and Others refers to the ongoing challenge of meeting the needs of the self, while also meeting the needs of others.

- **Self** covers the overarching human need to develop and express our individual self.

- **Others** reflects our need to make a difference and contribute in small and large ways so that we feel that our life has been worthwhile.

Keeping the balance between Self and Others is another universal and enduring theme in life:

> If I am not for myself, who will be for me? But if I am only for myself, who am I?
>
> Rabbi Hillel

Meaning is found in both Being and Doing and in both Self and Others and is lost when one is expressed at the exclusion of the other.

To check out this aspect of meaningful work we can ask:

- Do I often find myself resenting the demands of others?

- Can I easily speak from my point of view at work, or does the force of others, or the corporate culture, divorce me from myself?

Tensions are part of the ongoing dynamic of creating a meaningful life and meaningful work. By attending to them, noticing when different dimensions of meaning are becoming unbalanced for us (often signalled by strong feelings, upset or a noticeable loss of interest in something), we can examine and decide what to do to restore balance, and therefore meaning. In Chapter 4 we will come back to the tensions and also show the implications of when tensions are not addressed (over time).

Inspiration and Reality of Self and Circumstances

Here we focus on the bigger realm in which meaningfulness takes place, which is, at any time, somewhere between Inspiration and Reality; between our hopes, ideals and visions for the future and the place in which we currently find ourselves. Between heaven and earth, the profound and the profane. In work it is often noticed by one person describing a vision for the future and another saying 'let's get real', one person starting sentences with 'would it be possible to...' and another with 'but in reality...'. Both are automatically present in conversations about meaningfulness. The important point here is that meaning gets lost if we only focus on inspiration, and work becomes ungrounded and pollyannaish, but meaning also gets lost when we only focus on reality, and work becomes without hope for the future.

Inspiration

Meaningfulness is experienced when a person feels aligned with some form of ideal. This could be drawn from religious sources, our relations with other people, strongly held principles or nature.

People in workshops spoke about Inspiration in the following ways:

* vision of a possible future;

* a bigger purpose for it all;

* family;

* love;

* the order that underpins the universe;

* following the vision in my heart;

* grace;

* doors opening.

An example of how people experienced this at work: 'We decided to start the meetings with prayers or any text that has inspired a person, and this focus at the beginning lifted us above ourselves'.

Writings from all over the world are full of examples of the importance of inspiration and here are some:

The capacity for hope is the most significant fact of life. It provides human beings with a sense of destination and the energy to get started.

Norman Cousins

The world is: all that there is.

Buddha

Just living is not enough. One must have sunshine, freedom, and a little flower.

Hans Christian Andersen

Grace means more than gifts. In grace something is transcended, once and for all overcome. Grace happens in spite of something; it happens in spite of separateness and alienation. Grace means that life is once again united with life, self is reconciled with self. Grace means accepting the abandoned one. Grace transforms fate into a meaningful vocation. It transforms guilt to trust and courage. The word grace has something triumphant in it.

Yrjö Kallinen

You can't wait for inspiration. You have to go after it with a club.

Jack London

I keep my ideals, because in spite of everything I still believe that people are really good at heart.

Anne Frank

Hope is the thing with feathers / That perches in the soul, / And sings the tune without the words / And never stops at all.

Emily Dickinson, *Complete Poems*, 32

Yet, though there is much written about inspiration, at times we feel anything but inspired. Here are some questions you might ask to check on how inspired you are feeling at work?

- Do I feel uplifted at work?

- Does my work make me feel hopeful about the future?

- Do I have a vision for my work?

- Do I experience a connection with the spirit at work?

- What nourishes and centres me at work?

- What gives life to my work?

- How does our organisation generate inspiration? What destroys it?

- What keeps my heart open when so much could make me cynical?

Reality of Self and Circumstances

Meaningfulness cannot be experienced when we pretend, either in relation to ourselves or to our circumstances. It includes awareness that we are imperfect and live in an imperfect world. It can come from being able to discern the reality of what is happening in an organisation. It refers to a desire for authenticity and the truth, a need to be treated as adult.

People in workshops spoke about Reality of Self and Circumstances in the following ways:

- being genuine;

- coming to grips with what is;

- a kite flies best against the wind;

- breakdowns lead to breakthroughs;

- disturbance and desire;

- when we are out of alignment with our authentic self, we experience dis-ease;

- allow the ebb and flow;

- real;

- grounded;

- not Pollyannaish;

- grist to the mill;

- genuine;

- not pretending.

Examples from the workplace are: 'There is nothing wrong with all of this mission and vision and values stuff in itself. However, if we are not allowed to articulate where we do not and cannot live up to this, it feels as if we mock something that is really quite profound'; 'When I read some of our ads, or value statements I think, "This is partly true"; this is a good company. But every time we overstate, we also lose a little of ourselves in the process. It has to be grounded'.

Again, the importance of facing reality is an enduring and universal theme for human beings:

> Weeds are so interwoven with the grain that we would, at the same time as ripping out the weeds, also remove the grain. Who wants to be without fault, rips out her passion and destroys with her weakness also her strength.
>
> Source unknown

> Nothing but that which profiteth them can befall my loved ones.
>
> Baha'u'llah

> We cannot experience true community if we do not dare to ask difficult and pertinent questions. Similarly for employees it often provides a lot of freedom and creativity to articulate an unsolvable problem and for this to be recognised by leadership.
>
> Willem de Liefde

> The art of living lies less in eliminating our troubles than in growing with them.
>
> Bernard M. Baruch

> You mustn't be frightened if a sadness rises in front of you, larger than any you have ever seen; if an anxiety, like light and cloud-shadows, moves over your hands and over everything you do. You must realise that something is happening to you, that life has not forgotten you, that it holds you in its hand and will not let you fall.
>
> Rainer Maria Rilke

> To change one's life is not to change our outer circumstances: it is to change one's reactions.
>
> Gurdjieff

> When I hear somebody sigh, 'Life is hard,' I am always tempted to ask, 'Compared to what?'
>
> Sydney J. Harris

Sometimes it seems that we never stop facing reality, but at other times it is useful to check on how real we are being:

- Do we face up to reality at work, or is 'reality' all there is?

- Are we tolerant of being human?

- Do we recognise that life is messy and is that OK?

- At work, can we openly discuss when we do not live up to our values?

The dynamic dance between Inspiration and Reality is also a universal and ancient theme:

> To succeed in life, you need three things: a wishbone, a backbone and a funny bone.
>
> Reba McEntire

> Reality can be beaten with enough imagination.
>
> Author unknown

> Reality leaves a lot to the imagination.
>
> John Lennon

> The real voyage of discovery consists of not in seeking new landscapes but in having new eyes.
>
> Marcel Proust

> What we achieve inwardly will change outer reality.
>
> Otto Rank

> Reality is that which, when you stop believing in it, doesn't go away.
>
> Philip K. Dick

> No man will be found in whose mind airy notions do not sometimes tyrannize, and force him to hope or fear beyond the limits of sober probability.
>
> Samuel Johnson

> I have a very firm grasp on reality! I can reach out and strangle it any time!
>
> Author unknown

Summary

In this chapter we have shown how the Map of Meaning came into being, what its various elements mean and how they relate to each other. We have also shown how the elements of the Map are not only supported by our research but also form enduring and universal themes in our quest to be fully human. To understand meaningfulness and its impact on us, it is useful to tease apart the strands that make up the whole, as we have done in this chapter. At the same time the different parts clearly relate to each other. In our experience it is how all these elements play out dynamically as we live our life that truly provides the experience of meaning. In the following chapters we show how the Map can help us talk about and make decisions based on meaning and how we can take charge of meaning in our lives so that it can lead to an increased experience of meaningfulness.

Part 1
Taking personal responsibility for meaningful work

This part of the book helps you to stand firmly in your own meaning and to stay in charge of what creates meaning for you.

We start with the personal, because meaning is deeply personal. Only you can decide what makes your life worth living and what you will do to generate meaning in your life and work. Only you know when an absence of meaning needs to be taken seriously. Only you can find the courage to live meaningfully and it is you who experiences the joy from doing so.

Your work, and how you speak to others about it, reflects back to who you are, the career choices you make, what you have settled for, what you are creating, or challenging, and what you rejoice in, or which battles you have decided to let go. While work plays a part in shaping our destiny and takes place within large, complex and often seemingly intractable systems, it is also made up of the daily choices that we make. These choices create who each of us is becoming, as well as shaping the experience of life and work we have.

As we make clear in the second part of this book, organisations can and do play a significant role in the extent to which you are able to experience meaningful work. But in organisational life we find that the first step towards collectively creating meaningful work begins with each individual worker reconnecting to what, for them, is meaningful.

It is precisely because organisational practices and personal work habits can distract us from working meaningfully that we need to be clear what is important to us and take responsibility for it. It is true that some people have more power than others and that this might impact their ability to create or experience meaningful work. It is also the case that it is easier to stay true to ourselves in some organisations than it is in others. This is dependent on the structure, culture and purpose of the organisation in which you work and we will look at these in Part 2.

We have, however, seen time and again that those who become clear on what is meaningful to them, and learn how to speak about this with others, have been able to actively shape their work and lives to be more meaningful. And, that they have also become more effective at work as they learn to speak to purpose.

You may read this book for yourself, or because as a leader or consultant, teacher or parent, you want to help others to work and live meaningfully. However, it is still important to apply the learning of this book to yourself first. This honours the innate equality in human relationships as co-searchers for meaning. And you then speak from a shared experience of using the Map rather than inflicting a tool on the other person. It will also help you to learn effective ways of using it for yourself, which you can share with others.

In this first part of the book we therefore look at what is meaningful to you and how you can strengthen and develop this.

The chapters in this section follow a pattern. We start by introducing an exercise so that you can experience for yourself how using the Map can make a difference in your life. Next we write about our observations from working with the Map.

This will help you understand not only how to increase meaningful living and work for yourself, but also how to use the Map of Meaning with others. Finally, by reviewing the work of others, we aim to enrich your understanding of a specific aspect of meaningfulness, so you can refer to the ideas, theories and research that show the intellectual foundations and rigour of the Map of Meaning.

3

Talking about meaning at the most accessible level

The big question of 'What is the meaning of life?' often seems too complex to engage with and too far removed from our daily reality; something best left to philosophers and theologians. Yet it is in that daily reality, in the choices we make, the people we connect with and the actions we take that we create a meaningful life. To create a strong connection between the big questions and our day-to-day realities we need a simple way to understand and say to ourselves and others what is meaningful to us.

In this chapter we show in detail how the Map of Meaning helps give words to our sense of meaning, so that we can think and speak clearly about the things we feel deeply and know are important to us. We also show how the Map helps us to talk easily with others about meaning in a way that is grounded and engaging, and that also draws out what others hold as meaningful, so we can transcend our different perspectives. To help you begin to work with the Map of Meaning, we have included detailed exercises in each chapter, with instructions and post-exercise discussions. These have immeasurably helped people both understand and use the Map, make changes in their own life and work, and assist others. So we encourage you to begin doing the exercises straight away. You can come back to them, as many have, when times and circumstances may have changed.

Making meaning visible to yourself

To start, we invite you to work with the Map in order to become more familiar with your own inner meanings and the ways you express these. If you need to be reminded of the descriptors of each of the dimensions of meaningful work please refer to the previous chapter.

Exercise 3.1 is the first of many exercises that feature in the remaining chapters. You will find in Appendices 2 and 3 two versions of the Map of Meaning. One has just the main elements named on it, while the other has just the structure and no words. Work with the version that seems to you best fitted to the exercise.

Exercise 3.1

Purpose

Finding your way into the world of meaning.

Instructions

• First, ask yourself, 'What did I do, or experience, in my work in the past week that was deeply meaningful to me?' (Check your diary if you need to remind yourself what you've been doing.)

• Please write this down.

• Now take a copy of the Map (see Appendix 2 or 3) and write down your answers to these questions where you think they belong:

• In Unity with Others what did I experience that was meaningful to me? What was meaningful in Service to Others, Expressing Full Potential and Integrity with Self?

Doing Exercise 3.1 might help you recognise some of the pathways to meaningfulness that are present in your life but that you haven't noticed until now. You may see activities in a new light. For example, you might notice how a coffee with a colleague is not 'avoiding work' or even 'taking a well-earned break', but rather that it provides a real source of meaning for you both (Unity with Others). Or you may recall that in a certain situation you acted more courageously than you have before and that this is an expression of Integrity with Self. Give yourself a little time to reflect on what you have noticed.

What we have learned

The importance of making meaning present to ourselves

One of the most valuable aspects of working with the Map is that it helps people find words to talk about what is deeply important in their lives. When we do not have these words meaning is just another emotion in a range of emotions we experience throughout any day. As one participant said, 'We know when we have meaning and we know when we have lost it. It makes such a difference *to see it outside ourselves* and give it words, rather than just experience it as a feeling'.

Words come quite readily to people once, through the four pathways they break down the bigger questions into more accessible ones. Giving specific words to where we experience meaning enables us to consciously notice where we have and do not have meaning in our lives rather than abandoning it to others, thinking it has nothing to do with us or feeling inadequate when such topics are discussed. It helps us to see that meaning-making is a natural, everyday human activity, done by ordinary people just like us. The profound is not necessarily abstract and complex but is grounded and simple.

If meaning is so natural, why is it so hard to put into words?

In our research and work we consistently experience the deep engagement ordinary human beings have with meaning. This begs the question: If meaning is so natural to being human, and often so strongly felt, why do we find it so hard to talk about?

One of the most well-known and well-referenced theories on meaningful life is logotherapy, developed by Victor Frankl (Frankl 1963). His work arose from his experience in a concentration camp, where he found that even in such terrible conditions human beings still have 'a will to meaning'. While this desire for meaningfulness is innate to being human, Frankl argues that it is futile to look for THE meaning of life because the answer may well be impossible to find. He suggests that a more useful way of putting the question is, 'What does life expect from the individual, now, today and tomorrow?' Life, in this sense, does not mean something vague, but something very real and concrete. The bigger question is translated into more immediate questions of 'Why am I doing this? Why am I living my life this way, taking this path and not some other?' (Court 2004). This is precisely what the Map helps us do.

We ask 'What is meaningful about your work, over the last ten years, the last week, today?' In engaging with these questions, people start to make finer and finer distinctions between where their work is meaningful, where work is neither here nor there and where it is demoralising or demeaning. We find that when they have this focused way of expressing personal meaning they often comment that they had 'known this all along' and experience this reclaimed knowledge as particularly powerful and fulfilling.

Coming home to ourselves

'I trust this because I recognise it. It is like coming home, coming to a very familiar, strong, safe and peaceful place'.

What we have noticed is that many people, when they first reconnect with their own meanings in working with the Map, have this strong sense of coming home. Like any homecoming this is empowering, but can also be emotional and sometimes a little uncomfortable. People may be moved, joyful or sad. One person said, 'I no longer feel a lost soul. I have found myself again'. Another said, 'I can see how step by step I can reclaim the inner territory of myself'.

The soul, 'the inner space in each of us', which has longed for us to return, feels complete. The deeper significance of this, as one colleague who regularly works with the Map points out, is that:

> In coming home to ourselves we also come home into the world.
> We belong in the world. But how can we claim and stand in our
> citizenship of the world without being at home in ourselves?

We live at a time where the pace of life and work has accelerated and this pulls our focus outwards. The ability to be close to ourselves is easily lost and we can forget what is important. Knowing what is meaningful helps us to put boundaries between our self and our work, and be discerning about what is happening to us as human beings. Working with the Map helps us to hold strong to what we know. Having our feet grounded in our own being and meanings allows us to more fully express our commitment, to ourselves, to others and to life. And also make thoughtful decisions about what we no longer want to put our energy towards.

Having an inner place to dwell provides continuity in a world of change. Over time we can build a sense of permanence in ourselves where we can stand firm in relation to the emotions of others, changes that take place in our organisations and things that challenge and frighten us. One workshop participant said:

My job was radically re-engineered and during that time I stuck a copy of the Map on the wall above my desk. It helped me to stay focused on what is important to me in the job and also to speak up if something that was important to me, such as having time to have a conversation with my clients, threatened to be engineered out of the window.

Standing strong in your own language

Words are not neutral; the same word has different connotations for different people. To keep meaningfulness close to you (that is, to be strong in yourself while you engage with others), it is important that you use language that resonates with you.

You may have found that some of the labels for the four pathways are natural for you, whereas others may sit less comfortably. For example, Unity with Others may work for you or it may imply conformity. Integrity with Self may not work for you because you believe that the self, or ego, must get out of the way rather than be focused on. Some people replace Integrity with Self by 'becoming my true self' or 'developing my conscious self' or 'who I am on the inside'. Meanings may have been 'given' to us, by family, culture, work or faith. Because of these deeply seated roots, we may have strong feelings about them. So, a person might say 'I hate "service". That word always makes me feel guilty. But it is important to me to contribute and make a difference'.

In the next exercise we suggest you first ask yourself, for each of the pathways, why is this important to me? and then, what do I believe about this? From there you can select the words that most accurately express your truths.

As you do this exercise, keep to the structure of the Map and create a version that is based on the words that are close to your heart and that are based on your own beliefs. These can be directly from you, ancient wisdom, religious sayings, fridge magnets, family lore or anything else that has resonated enough for you to remember. As you can see from the examples in the exercise below, meaning may also be influenced by your current experience (e.g. I do not want to be washed away) or it may be a belief that you have carried with you for many years.

Exercise 3.2

Purpose

To own the Map of Meaning and your own beliefs.

Instructions

- Choose a copy of the Map of Meaning (Appendix 2 or 3).
- In each of the four pathways, write down a phrase or two that sum up the meaning of this pathway to you. For example, here are some phrases that others have put in Integrity with Self:
  - You must be the change you want to see in the world.
  - I need to know who I am in relation to the world.
  - I do not want to be washed away by others.
  - Getting to my true (higher) self.
- Put your words in each of the four pathways and replace any labels in the Map that you feel you need to change.

People have sometimes noticed that, while they have plenty of phrases for one pathway, they struggle to find a phrase for another or are dissatisfied with what they write down. For others, permission to find the word that's 'right' for them releases a deep flow of meaning. In this sense the Map helps us be the authors of our own view of the world, and therefore authorise ourselves.

You'll also see that each of the statements in the example not only describes a pathway but also says something about the beliefs that underpin it. So you can use this exercise to clarify what you believe and then connect these beliefs to how you live your daily life. For example, one person wrote, 'I believe that who I am becoming as a result of my work is as important as what I achieve'. This came from examining her statement, 'I don't want to be washed away by others', and led her to develop skills in standing more strongly for what really mattered to her. Another cited something he had once read: 'True loss is a life spent in ignorance of one's true self', and realised that he needed to find ways to increase his insight into himself. It is this underpinning belief that connects you to the pathway and, ultimately, supports you taking action to living a meaningful life.

What we have learned about introducing people to the Map

Working with what we hold to be meaningful

Consciously exploring, questioning and examining, we can begin to pay attention to meaning. This helps us decide whether to keep, discard or alter meanings over time. In the future if you find life a bit meaningless, you might wish to revisit Exercise 3.2 to check and possibly revitalise what might now have become hollow or formulaic phrases. Voicing our meanings, the things that make our life worth living, is an essential skill because it helps us to see that meaning is not just something that is waiting for us. A meaningful life is something we constantly create.

Once people consciously come home to what they have 'always known', their relationship to themselves changes. There's a sense that what they have always known needs to be taken seriously and treated responsibly. They can take stock and see where their world-views and beliefs have been put into action and where they have not. After doing Exercise 3.2, a participant said:

> What I see is that I've believed for years that Unity with Others is really important for me, but what am I doing about it? Where do I find support? Where do I seek companionship? Just believing this is not enough. I need to put my beliefs into action, or it's all just words. I'm going to put the Map up in my home office and on the fridge to remind me that the things I believe should guide my actions every day.

While coming home to ourselves may increase our feeling of solidity, and give us more energy to act in alignment with our beliefs, how safe does it feel to speak about meaning to other people? How does working with the Map affect our shared experience of meaning?

Voicing meaning: changing the way we relate to each other

Margaret Wheatley (2002) writes that when we sit together and talk about what's important to us, we become alive. In this section we focus on making meaningfulness present in conversation. The context in which you first start using the Map does not matter. It can be with a family member, neighbour, a colleague, someone you work with in your local community. The key is to learn to share and speak about what is meaningful, and to learn to listen to others as 'meaning-full' beings; to understand that each person has had many experiences that help them know what makes their work and personal lives feel worthwhile.

Exercise 3.3

Purpose

To practise deliberately bringing meaning into the conversation.

Instructions

- With another person – a friend, partner, colleague – place a copy of the Map in a place (on the table, the couch or the wall) where you can both see it.

- Take your time, go through each of the elements of the Map and ask the other person, 'In Unity with Others, what have been some of your rewarding or enriching (use any word you like here but frame in a positive way) experiences over the last month (week, year)?'

You can make the exercise more specific if, for example, you want to evaluate a particular relationship. So, you may ask, 'In Unity with Others, what do you think we have done particularly well in our marriage/partnership, mother/daughter relationship, group or team over the past year? In Service to Others?' Go on around the remaining pathways.

Comments people made after doing this exercise included: 'It was a really good place to listen from, a place to stand for the richness and the possibility of the other person' and 'In evaluating our relationship from a profound place we realised how simple it was to actually talk about what is important to us, and how little we do it'. One person doing the exercise in a family context said:

> The deeper meanings gave us a creative place to plan from. In Unity with Others, we identified that we had not been proactive in our social lives lately even though spending time with friends and family is really meaningful to us. So it was easy to identify some actions starting with some simple phone calls to catch up.

Another person used the Map with a colleague to give meaning to a task that was feeling overwhelming and unengaging:

We were preparing a workshop. We used the Map of Meaning to check in with each other around it, to focus on how we wanted the day to be and what we wanted for us from doing this work.

It helped us connect into the reason we were doing the workshop in the first place. This re-energised us at a time when putting together the last bits felt like a hard slog. It helped us stay connected to the meaning the work had, and also helped us support each other. And it created something we can go back to when the work gets tough.

What we have learned

Not only does the Map help us make the inner world of meaning visible to ourselves, it gives us practical ways to own these meanings and share them with others. This helps us to take something private into the public domain. Only when it is in the public domain, can it drive meaningful changes or help us preserve what we collectively agree to be meaningful.

Sharing meaning in a professional group

Once we know our own life meanings and have learned to discuss these with others in a safe context, it might be time to find out how voicing meaning can affect group situations. This exercise can be used for any group, work team, voluntary group, organising committee or school board that is asking itself questions such as: What is it all for? What is our purpose here? What is at the foundation of our collective decision-making? How do we connect ourselves to the values of this organisation? Or, How shall we plan for next year?

Exercise 3.4

Purpose

To see the other as a 'meaning-full' human being.

Instructions

- Put eight sheets of paper around the room (on walls or any other place where they can be easily read).
- Head each of these with one of the elements of the Map: Service to Others, Inspiration, Reality of Self and Circumstances, Integrity with Self, Expressing Full

Potential, Unity with Others, Being/Doing, Self/Others. Also provide an empty sheet in which people can add anything meaningful to them that is not adequately captured in the Map.

- Ask participants to go around the room and write down what they already *believe* about the importance of each of the elements of the Map (You can also put this as 'what they hold dear' or 'already know' about the importance of each of the elements to them.) Make sure that they do not add their names to what they have written. Give examples such as 'In a previous exercise people wrote down under Integrity with Self such things as "you need to be the change you want to be in the world" '. (There are many examples for all the pathways in Chapter 2.)

- It's important that people feel free to write down anything that comes to mind. This can be wisdom from a parent, something they just know/believe, a religious text or a Yogi Berra quote, as long as it is meaningful to them.

- Once everyone has written something down, ask the participants to go quietly around the room and read what everyone has written.

- Then ask people to reflect individually on what they observed and, if they wish, to discuss this in pairs or as a group.

The first thing we have noticed when everyone is moving around the room is the respectful silence. As one of the participants said: 'There was a subtle change in the energy of the room as we started to see each other as "meaning-full" beings'.

Another participant said: 'Of course I knew that other people must also contemplate the meaning of life, but to so clearly and immediately see the evidence that I am not alone in this is deeply moving. The depth and breadth of all of the comments really struck me'.

In a team environment participants comment on how using the Map enables and legitimises the topic of meaningfulness in the conversation:

> Having the Map present, and being told that human beings know what is intrinsically meaningful to them, meant that I did not have to think about how my beliefs came across. I could simply write them down in the knowledge that others would do the same. It also did not feel too risky or self-revealing because the process allowed for a certain amount of anonymity.

What we have learned

Creating a grounded and safe space to talk about what's important

The Map, provides a neutral space where people hear themselves and each other easily speak about meaning. At this very basic level, it provides a place where meaning can be expressed and reflected on before people need to consider anything else.

The Map legitimises conversations about meaning. It puts meaningfulness 'out there, and shared' instead of just 'in here'. It makes our inner world visible in a way that makes it safe because we are not alone.

Shared meaning: identifying our commonalities, while also acknowledging our differences

Of course, meaning is subjective. The significance we assign to something is dependent on the world-views we have, and these vary widely. This has been used as an excuse to 'just not go there'. This ignores the fact that we act from common meanings every day and that in order to act collectively it is also important to talk collectively, regardless of the differences that exist among individuals, cultures or groups. We found that the Map, because the dimensions are shared and so easily understood, is an excellent tool for people to recognise and act on commonalities, while (because they are invited to use their own language, representative of their experiences and culture) respecting the differences of world-views.

Exercise 3.5

Purpose

In this exercise we explore the very real differences that can arise when people share what is meaningful to them.

Instructions

- Continue with Exercise 3.4 and ask the people involved to look at the sheets on the wall and note the language that has been used.

- What do they notice that they have in common? What is different?

- Ask them to discuss what they observed, in pairs or in a small group.
- If you did the exercise in a pair but are also intending to use it with a group you might also want to notice the difference in language that each of you used.

What we have learned

Noticing our similarities, while being safe enough to enjoy our differences

In labelling the parts of the Map we deliberately chose words that are big enough for individuals to see where they connect. In other words, I might say 'teamwork' and you might say 'that's too much of a business word to me and I want to use "love"', and a third person might say 'that is too touchy-feely for me and I would say it is about supporting each other'. The label Unity with Others was chosen because it captures in the broadest sense the shared dimension of meaningfulness that is experienced through quality relationships.

When the common dimensions of meaning are identified, the Map and the way we work with it makes it immediately obvious that when we move from the abstract to the concrete, people have very diverse world-views and experiences. The shared framework helps to generate enough commonality to also help people to see that not everyone has the same paradigm as them. This makes it easier to have conversations about differences without making anyone wrong and provides the possibility for enquiry. The Map does not privilege one world-view over another. It therefore helps us to be skilful in holding our view peacefully, staying constructive in the midst of contrasting world-views, remaining open to the possibility of change and creating space for those who do not wish to participate in conversations involving, for example, spirituality or religion. As one of the participants in our research said:

> The Map allows the possibility of moving meaning and purpose from a purely individualised focus into a place where it is shared and therefore collective, while also retaining an individual connection and expression. Because of this the Map allows us to engage with the potentially divisive topic of meaning in ways that allow a greater recognition of what we have in common than what is different.

Identifying common purposes provides the basis for shared meaning and hence purposeful collective action that (because it is intimately linked to personal meaning and language) also engages the heart of each individual. Another participant went on to say:

> Given that we can distinguish what we have in common, it allows us to place this at the foundation of what we hold important and then to hold to this as a group when challenged. Connectivity is stronger when there is an emotional bond so involving people – sharing meaning with people – creates a much stronger bond.

On the basis of these deep meanings that have now been made visible, the group can decide what to do, and what to stop doing, in order to increase meaning. You can find more examples of how groups have done this in the second half of the book.

Treating each other as meaningful human beings

The question of 'How do I live a meaningful life?' is not separate from our relationships with others. The question does not only pose 'What happens if I treat myself as a deeply meaningful being?' but also 'What happens if we treat each other as deeply meaningful beings? What if we treated our family members and colleagues as deeply meaningful beings? What if we treated those who are managed by us, and those who manage us, as meaningful human beings?'

We are all used to hearing colleagues say, 'Why are they asking us to do this? It's entirely pointless'; or, 'I've lost any spark of enthusiasm for this project'; or, 'No one seems to appreciate my ideas'. These comments can often have the effect of intensifying our own sense of meaninglessness, but with an awareness of the Map it is easier to hear these comments as a yearning for making a difference, or for inspiration, or for expressing full potential. Now we can respond more constructively, and retain our own sense of meaningfulness, in the face of these remarks rather than slide into a gripe session, as one long-term user of the Map describes:

> Now I also know that this person, whatever they are saying or doing, is also searching for meaning. It helps me feel a compassionate connection to them and listen practically to what they're saying with the Map in mind. Often I can recognise an expression of longing for a deep alignment with others, or a frustration at not being able to express their full potential. At my best I can ask a well-framed question that can help them see a new way forward, but

even listening like this makes a difference because it stops me from
plummeting with them into negativity.

What others have written about the challenges and possibilities of voicing meaning in relationships

'Human existence is in essence dialogical' (Frankl 1963). 'Human beings need
and actively seek out dialogue and encounter with the world, with others and
themselves. To this end, the individual and the world are inextricably linked'
(Sykes 2007: 1, 349). 'As we talk we construct the world we live in, and how
we talk changes that world' (Cooperrider and Whitney 2005). O'Reilley (1998)
talks about 'listening each other's souls into existence'.

This points to the power of shared speaking and listening as the way in
which we both create our personal and collective reality as well as our
individual sense of self. Once again we see the importance of talking about
what is deeply significant to us because it is part of creating a meaningful reality for ourselves and others. It is important to find the support that
comes from such conversations because we can often forget that a source of
true contentment and well-being is simply to 'turn to each other' (Wheatley
2002).

At the same time the fact that speaking to meaning is difficult has always
been recognised: 'There is a tendency to leave it [meaningfulness] unex-
plained or vague, as if everyone knows what it is but no one can put it into
words' (Overell 2009: 5).

But Carl Rogers argues powerfully for the transformative power of what can
happen between people when meaningfulness is voiced:

> It is the relationship itself that cures . . . Only by willing to be one's
> self within the relationship, by accepting one's own difference and
> having it accepted by another, can one discover the creativity and
> strength to change . . . At the foundation of human relations stands
> the ability to see each other as meaningful beings, to value the true
> humanity of each other. Not listen to each other as a technique of
> 'impression management' but as an empathic way of being present
> to the whole of the possibility of that person as a meaningful being.
>
> Rogers, cited in Pauchant 1995: 202

Voicing meaning to another clarifies, develops and enriches meaning,
often for both parties or, if done in a group, for all involved.

Understanding the vital role of meaning and being able to talk about it is
an essential part of being able to have meaningful relationships. Given that
we relate to things, people and events through their meaning for us, if we

are detached from meaning, we are also detached from a constructive relationship.

Martin Buber (1970) writes about the distinction between seeing people and their issues as I–It or I–Thou. In an I–It relationship, people are used as a goal, a tool for getting somewhere; people compete with each other for attention and become defined by their smallest selves. In the I–Thou relationship, concerns of time, space and cause are replaced by a concern for who the other really is as a human being. Buber writes that in essence this relationship is the most simple and mutual, because it preserves individual awareness and integrity while also seeing the other person as being wholly whole and purposeful. Of course the I–It and I–Thou ways of relating wax and wane during a day but the possibilities of I–Thou relationships are greatly enhanced by the ability to see each other as meaningful beings.

Our experience with the Map of Meaning is that it greatly assists us to have what Martin Buber calls I–Thou relations and to sustain them over time. This offers something of real value in organisations where the general discourse is often hijacked by 'hard' management, at the expense of who we truly are as managers and employees. This has profound implications for our human ability to address issues of meaning at work. And therefore also for our motivation, well-being and creativity.

Summary

In this chapter we looked at the importance of voicing meaning and how to do so to ourselves and to others. We discussed several key ideas.

- In order to live meaningfully we need to be able to put words to our experience of meaning. This ability takes meaning from a vague yearning, or strong feelings, into something that is concrete and for which we can become responsible. The words we use for meaning need to resonate with our deeply held beliefs about life. The Map helps us be the authors of our own view of the world, and therefore authorise ourselves. Once we have these words we can think and speak clearly about the things we feel deeply and know are important to us, and we can go on to examine and be responsible for our beliefs and actions.

- If we want to live meaningfully it is essential to be able to effectively communicate to others what we hold deeply. It helps to become skilled at talking easily with others about meaning in a way that is grounded, and easy to listen to while seeing others as meaningful human beings. To practically implement this, it is valuable to learn how to listen for meaning in others, and to help them draw out what is meaningful to them.

- We live in a time where articulating and creating meaning requires all people in the organisation to be able to speak about what is meaningful to them. What humanity holds to be meaningful transcends our different perspectives and world-views. At the same time it is based on widely divergent spiritual and personal beliefs. The Map provides a neutral space where people hear themselves and each other easily speak about meaning. It allows for the possibility to meet and consult at a deep level.

- Living and working meaningfully is both a personal and socio-political choice. At a personal level, meaning is not passively received, but actively created. To be purposeful about creating meaning, we need to be able to give it words. Creating meaning is not a one-off decision, but rather an ongoing cycle of reflection and action in a world that often distracts us from what is most important to us. The Map helps to keep that which is most important to us at the forefront of our heart and mind. When we know what is meaningful to us we are stronger and more effective in communicating why a particular change, practice or action is important to us. When we do this collectively, meaning is taken out of the private realm and becomes a driver for social change. For this to happen, meaning needs to be demystified, shared and legitimately raised, and this is what the Map enables.

Once we have language that can powerfully raise our human concerns, how do we ensure that any actions we take continually support meaningful work? In the next chapter we show how to take the multiple dimensions of meaningful work into account in all our thinking and decisions.

4

Wholeness and integration
The relationship between the dimensions of meaning

Self *and* Other

> If I am not for myself, who will be for me? But if I am only for myself, what am I?
>
> Rabbi Hillel c.110 BC

Being *and* Doing

> When we abandon the creative tension between the contemplative and the active life both ends fly apart into madness. Action flies off into frenzy – a frantic and even violent effort to impose one's will on the world, or at least to survive against the odds. Contemplation flies off into escapism – a flight from the world into a realm of false bliss.
>
> Palmer 2004: 15

In the previous chapter we explored the importance of having words to express what we already 'know' and showed how this helps us come home to and stay strong in ourselves, recognise others as meaningful beings, have meaningful conversations and initiate meaningful action. In this chapter we discuss how the different pathways to meaning relate to each other and how life and work are more meaningful when we fill our time with all four dimensions of the Map.

The multiple dimensions of meaningful work are often experienced as tensions. When, over time, tensions cannot be reconciled, we experience greater sense of fragmentation and loss of meaning. When they can be reconciled it leads to greater harmony and increased meaningfulness. This is because:

- the different dimensions of meaningful work strengthen each other, so for example, Grant (2007) found that those who show the most prosocial behaviour at work (Serving Others) were also supported by high-quality relationships (Unity). And, if we want to help others, it is important to develop our own talents so we can do it effectively.

- meaning is lost when some dimensions are expressed at the exclusion of others. For example, when Unity is expressed at the exclusion of Expressing Full Potential, we can lose our unique voice and with it the meaning, health and well-being that comes from both Integrity with Self and a full expression of our gifts.

- meaning is not experienced in isolation, and therefore unbalanced expressions of meaning lead not only to a loss of meaning for ourselves but also for others. We all know people who focus on ambitiously Expressing their Full Potential but not on Unity with Others, thus impoverishing, slowing down or splitting the team.

It is therefore important to be able, as much as possible, to express all dimensions of meaning at the same time, either within one task or across a number of tasks within one job, or across our work and other life roles. We need to pay attention to the whole of our lives because when our lives are fragmented and unbalanced, over time we experience life as tiring, boring or chaotic, and generally meaningless. As one participant put it: 'I got burned out because I was constantly meeting people's demands; a whole lot of people's demands and suddenly everything got very bleak and empty. I had no time for myself'. Or another: 'We worked really well together, but I was no longer learning new things'.

Parker Palmer (2004) points out that we dislike holding the tension of conflicting demands and want 'to get on with it', because holding tension can be uncomfortable and we fear it can make us look uncertain and indecisive. In addition, in a time of accelerating pace of work and life, we may simply not have time to pay attention to such tensions.

Yet, when multiple meanings are all important, tensions inevitably arise. When these tensions are not noticed, or we can't find a way to easily reconcile them, we fall back on the most urgent or most comfortable (but not necessarily the most meaningful) thing to do. So, to fulfil our desire for meaning, we need to identify and express the four dimensions of meaning-ful work, while also finding ways of recognising and addressing their inherent tensions. This means adjusting our working patterns and life balance as part of an ongoing process of revisiting what really matters and who we want to become, a constant fine-tuning of our lives.

Paying attention to the relationship between the dimensions of meaningful work allows us to order our inner world – the home to which we have returned – and deliberately organise what is most important to us.

There is a lot of focus on 'balanced living' in self-help books and magazines, but this literature can be too simplistic. In essence much of this literature says: 'You need to decide what life roles and activities are important or enjoy-able to you and allocate the right amount of time to each of them and then "just do it"'. We found, however, that the tensions involved in living meaningfully lie deeper and are more complex than this type of solution suggests. Our research shows that it is the nature of being human to experi-ence constant tensions in our lives. We are not incompetent when we do not have balanced lives. The Map treats these tensions as a normal part of being human and makes them immediately visible. In the Map you see the tensions between 'Doing' and 'Being', as well as the tensions between 'Self' and 'Other' depicted by arrows that simultaneously pull us in opposing directions. Managing these is a bit like walking: a dynamic process of balancing many aspects of movement without falling forwards or backwards. The specific dimensions of the Map provide a very effective way of scanning for and noticing loss of balance, as well as intentionally increasing wholeness and integration.

In the first section of this chapter we look at how the tensions between 'Being' and 'Doing', 'Self' and 'Other' play out in our own lives. This helps us to notice our responses to them and any deep patterns and habits we may have formed.

In the second section of this chapter we return to the four pathways as a very practical way to work with the whole of meaning. Here we look at how the Map helps us to identify where we want to put our effort and energy, skills, talents and time, even when life pulls us in many different directions at once. We give a number of examples of how you can do this, and how you can assist others in doing this at an individual level. In Chapter 7 we look at what organisations can do to promote wholeness. There we discuss that loss of balance is not just an individual but also organisational concern, so, for example, a focus on service to others at the exclusion of unity can make customer service or community work quite meaningless.

As in the previous chapter, you will find a combination of exercises, ideas from others and practical case studies.

Recognising tensions as they play out in our lives

Is a balanced life a more meaningful life?

One of the questions that others have asked us, and we have asked ourselves, is whether a meaningful life is a balanced life. Many of the lives of extraordinary role models, such as Mandela, were not exactly balanced. In itself, we would argue, balancing does not generate meaning. As Pozzi and Williams (1998: 65) put it: 'Imagine your epitaph to read "she led a balanced life"'. But for us, ordinary humans, it is important to recognise that meaningfulness is found across the Map as a whole, and we all have examples of those who, at the end of their lives, wished they had been truer to themselves, more creative or playful with their talents, paid more attention to their relationships or made more of a difference, both inside and outside of work. In his commentaries on the writings of Gurdjieff and Ouspensky, Maurice Nicoll (1957) put it beautifully in saying that to be alive is to be present 'to every side of existence'. When we are present to every side of existence, the different dimensions strengthen each other. While we can consciously choose to spend a great deal of time and energy in one direction to accomplish something that is special or important to us, such as running a marathon, fostering children or getting to the next step on the career ladder, when it is no longer a conscious choice, or we feel we have no other options, or when we go on for too long and exclude other 'sides' of existence that also enrich our lives, we lose meaningfulness. In the following sections we explore the tensions more fully.

How the tensions between Being and Doing play out in our own lives

Exercise 4.1

Purpose

To explore the tensions between Being and Doing.

Instructions

- Go back and look at your response to Exercise 3.1 in Chapter 3. Now notice the amount that you have written down in the top two quadrants (Unity with Others, Integrity with Self) versus the bottom two. Look at how much time and energy you spend on Being versus Doing.

- Do you see a pattern? For example, do you see that you have spent too little time Being or too little time Doing? Have a look at a variety of life roles (parenting, community work, sport, etc.) and see whether you have followed a similar pattern. Where, for example, could you simply be content with being part of something and where did you need to direct things?

- What has been the impact of this and on whom?

- Is this a long-standing pattern or a new experience for you as the result of some shift in your life, such as retirement after a life of focused work? How does this pattern affect various aspects of your life, such as work, family, friends or leisure time?

- As you reflect on these tensions, what becomes apparent?

In Exercise 4.1 most people notice that they do not have enough time to 'be'; or that the way they are Being is not particularly meaningful. Some describe a pattern of running around and then collapsing in some sort of meaningless activity such as watching TV. Endless time can sink into pervasive modern technology. One person grieved over the lack of time she has for meditation (Being) compared to the demands of work and family (Doing). And many others echo how they have ignored various forms of Being: simply being with friends, being in nature (without always having to work in it), or paying attention to who our children are (becoming), just checking in with a colleague to see if they are okay. Or you may notice where you are developing skill at Being and the benefits you reap from this. One man who has always worked extremely hard was making some progress in his resolution to have 'quiet time with myself so that I can ponder on whether or not there is anything more than this life'. He noticed 'I am slowly moving out of work and into this. It's scary, but it has its lovely moments'. This exercise helped him to understand more clearly the role of Being in creating increasing meaningfulness.

Sometimes people notice that they have spent a lot of time Being but too little Doing. We can be prone to inertness and all know that without deadlines things would not get done. Some people found too little relationship between their Being and their Doing: 'I noticed that I had had the same goal for a long time and that I was spending a lot of time day-dreaming about it and discussing it with others. Putting it into action was frightening yet the only way to proceed'. Often people find long-standing patterns:

> I was part of a range of sports clubs and also, of course, of my family. Through this exercise, I found that wherever I was, I ended up being in charge of many things and enjoying few. I needed to learn to simply be with others and let others do more doing.

Taking the time to 'be' in our inner world allows us to explore it, to put what is inside 'out there' and understand and work with it. As one colleague said:

> People in the workshop could see their lives were unbalanced or that areas were unexplored and gained a sense of permission to focus their energy and questions in a different space in the Map. It helped to 'normalise' the discussion about unexplored, overdeveloped or unexpressed areas of our working life.

When they pay attention to tensions, people often uncover some deep-seated patterns in their lives. The following quote is from a research participant who, in her story, clearly identified the force of these patterns, in her case between Being and Doing:

> It has been a real battle with me regarding work because I felt my identity is so tied up with who I am in connection with my work; with the ability to earn a wage, with recognition from the world. It is so goal-oriented and I want to become process-oriented. I want to really let go and explore; be more open, more open to being able to respond in a more genuine way rather than what I see as a confined way. I accept that being employed does not necessarily mean I have to do it this way. It's just my experience of it and it's something that I see I need to address.

As we can see, these tensions are profound and not easily resolved. For example, overdeveloped 'goal orientation' can also affect other parts of our lives where we find we may spend much time Doing (e.g. running around attending various clubs and events) and little time Being (e.g. just sitting or reading, which are often times when our kids come to us with questions or just for a cuddle). Or running around so much at work that one's commitment to have an open door for colleagues becomes rather hollow. The issues that arise from such profound tensions are complex. Here we can only touch lightly on some of the main themes with regard to rebalancing Being and Doing that arose as we listened to people's stories over the years.

- Being is important, because the space of Being is often where the presence or absence of meaning is deeply felt.

- Both Being and Doing are features of our everyday personal and working lives; both pathways lead to meaningful living and working. Our contemplation directs our action; our action in turn feeds back to us who we are and what we have set out to do in the world.

- Outward movement (such as helping others) leads to inner development, and inner development (such as knowing oneself better) leads to more satisfying and effective outward movement.

- We need to become discerning about where we need to work with our being, stand back and not take action, and where we need to take action. The more skilful we become at this, the greater opportunity to increase our experience of meaningfulness.

- Joys and sorrows we never predicted enter our lives without warning, and the blessings we have today may be gone tomorrow. Thus, reflecting on where we need to just be, and where we need to do, can contribute to meaningfulness in ever-changing circumstances.

The tensions between Self and Others

The tensions between Self and Others has formed an ongoing theme in human experience and inquiry.

In what has been referred to as 'one of the most influential ideas in personality psychology today' (McAdams 1992: 340), Bakan (1966) introduces two concepts of 'agency' (Self) and 'communion' (Others), the tension between which he refers to as 'the basic duality of human existence'. Agency refers to the need for self-mastery, status, achievement and empowerment whereas communion refers to the need for love and friendship, dialogue, care and help, and community. Themes of agency are: self-esteem, self-confidence, strength and pride, and experiencing the self as an autonomous entity strong enough to cope with the situation at hand. It is therefore very important to us, not to see it as selfishness but rather as a healthy way of being human. Communion is about caring, belonging, making a difference, and intimacy. This other-direction too is therefore an essential part of being human. These themes of agency and communion are often seen as major organising principles in human life and at the same time as major tensions. When these tensions are not addressed, well-being is diminished (Fritz and Helgeson 1998). In addition, it has been found that meaning is lost when we experience what is referred to as unmitigated agency (agency at the expense of communion) or unmitigated communion (communion at the expense of agency) (Bakan 1966).

How the tensions between Self and Others may play out in our own lives

Exercise 4.2

Purpose

To explore the tensions between Self and Others.

Instructions

- Take a filled-out copy of the Map from a previous exercise.

- If you haven't got a filled-out copy, take an empty version (Appendix 2 or 3) and consider where in the past year you might have had tensions between your own needs and those of others. This can be between different roles (e.g. at home and at work) or within one role, or a combination of both. Fill these in on the copy of the Map if you wish.

- Or you may do this as a simple percentage of the time you spent in one side compared with time spent in another.

- Now consider the following questions. As an expression of tensions between Self and Others:

  - Notice how much you have written in the left-hand side (Integrity with Self, Expressing Full Potential) versus the right-hand side.

  - Do you see long-standing patterns across a variety of roles of this tension? What has been the impact of this?

  - Is this a new experience for you as the result of some shift or current focus in your life (e.g. a new baby or a new job)?

- What issues does this raise for you?

You may notice in doing Exercise 4.2 just how much time is spent caring for the needs of others, while your own are neglected. You may at this time, as with a new baby, be fine doing this, or you may, in terms of time spent increasingly at work or with your family, notice how resentful you feel. You may notice that you spend a lot of time in Unity with Others, as part of a large family or local, or cultural community, but you may question where you have followed you own pathway in life. Seeing this helped some people understand the causes of discomfort and diminished well-being. For example, one man felt that 'being a good Christian' required him to only serve others and not 'be selfish' by attending to his own needs. Working with the Map helped him to see that he had to listen to his son, who had been telling him for some years that he also needed to care of himself. Now he could see this as part of creating a healthier self, better able to serve others. He commented: 'My son will be very happy when I tell him what I have learned'.

You may find that everybody at work really likes you, but that you can't remember when you last spoke up for something that was important to you, where you set some boundaries around your availability or where someone actually covered a day's work for you rather than the other way around. Or, you may notice that you are very efficient, but don't have many day to day conversations with your workmates, or feel lonely or excluded at work.

For some, the different pathways bring up different emotions. In some cases people noticed that one area felt slightly uncomfortable for them and they didn't feel at ease in it, either because it is over- or under-developed. 'Oh, I don't want to go *there*!' said one person looking at the quadrant Service to Others. In her case, the word 'service' put her off, because of a family background in which women were supposed to be endlessly serving others. During the workshop she examined how she might like to contribute, free from the violent reaction in which her past experience trapped her.

Some people also find that their lives have become too much about themselves, their own financial security, their own freedom, intellectual development or creativity. Some find they are withdrawing from the world because it all feels too scary or overwhelming, but that this is still all about themselves.

Again, Self and Others strengthen each other. To feel hopeful about humanity, to feel in control of our destiny, to grow as human beings, self- and other-orientations need to be integrated over time. Here are some of the main themes with regard to rebalancing Self and Others that arose as we listened to people's stories over the years.

The tensions between uniqueness and belonging

People experience the excitement of being unique, independent and self-determining, of being responsible for themselves and having a strong sense of personal achievement and competence. At the same time they find deep and rich meaning in belonging to a group that shares values, interests and ways of doing things. But sometimes to belong (e.g. in a faith group) we may feel we have to suppress our own unique voice or accept that we bring only part of ourselves to a particular group. Sometimes in order to stay true to our own unique talents (e.g. holding a highly individual view as an artist) we might need to accept feelings of loneliness and separation from others

The tensions between giving and receiving

This is captured in the following story. 'Two years ago in my home town we set up a time bank. People offer skills and goods in exchange for someone else's skills and goods, without exchanging money. One of the unusual things noticed in the most recent evaluation of the time bank is that while most participants are very happy to give their time, they are very hesitant to ask others to do something for them'. This ultimately endangers the natural flow of giving and receiving, both of which make our lives meaningful. Another friend said recently: 'I just don't know how to receive'. Of course, some of you might also realise that the balance has recently been going too much the other way (e.g. your parents keep doing things for you and you don't have the time to reciprocate or even simply appreciate it).

The tension between taking responsibility and handing things over to a group

Here is an example of the way someone handled this tension. 'Recently someone told me about an incident at her school where parents were concerned about a matter. Her initial thought had been to take over and address the issue with the principal, but after some reflection on the right balance she decided to encourage the parents to gather and ask for their solutions'. In another example, a self-employed colleague without much paid work recently spent a lot of time working for a particular board she is on, because currently she has time to spare and others don't.

The tension of thinking for ourselves and accepting the wisdom of others

This tension centres on making decisions about which battles to fight, and which to let go; when to learn by listening and maybe see the limitations of our own point of view and when to hold to the importance of something we hold dear in the face of disagreement.

Neglected tensions

In this chapter we do not argue that a meaningful life is a fully balanced life. However, if there are long-standing patterns of imbalance, this can cause a sense of meaninglessness.

In mapping out the time and energy you spend in each dimension, it is easy to understand why you may still experience a sense of meaninglessness even though your life is rich and full, and even though one dimension still has profound meaning for you.

Figure 4.1 **Integrated versus unmitigated expressions of meaningful work**

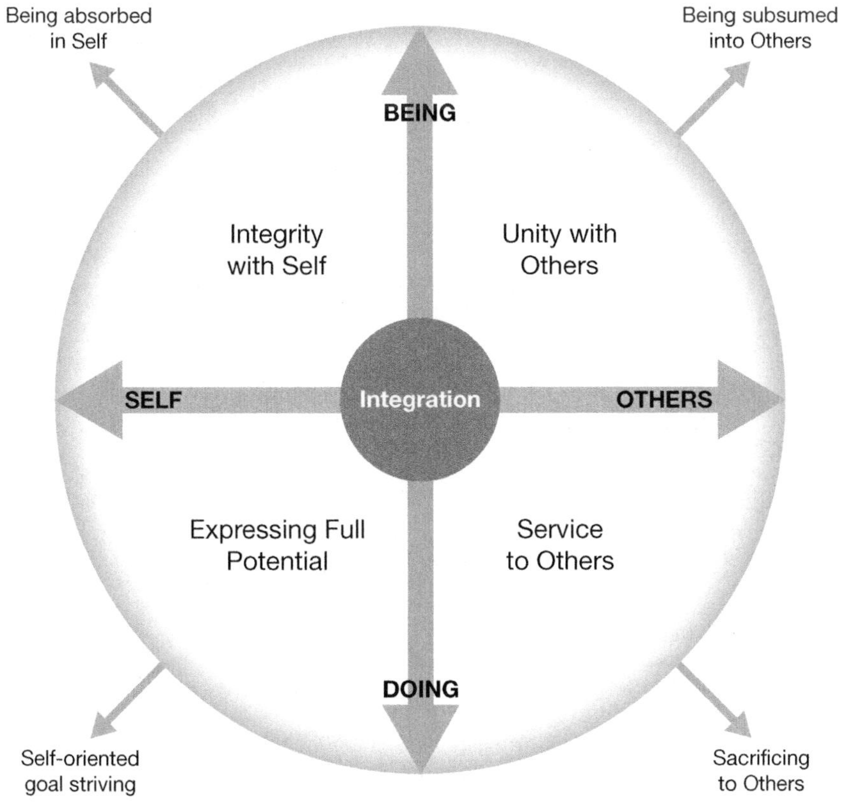

Your energies might simply have been directed lopsidedly for too long. In Figure 4.1 we offer another version of the Map of Meaning, but this time one which shows both integrated and unmitigated dimensions of meaning. Unmitigated is where one dimension is expressed, over too long a period of time, at the exclusion of another. As one dimension grows too strong, one or more other dimensions of the Map become neglected. The words on the outside of the Map are those we use for overdeveloped meanings.

In Table 4.1 we have summed up the effects of too much, or too little, focus on the different dimensions.

Table 4.1 **Effects of unmitigated expressions of Meaningful Work**

Integrity with Self	**Unity with Others**
Self-Absorption occurs when there is too *much* focus on the self, which can lead to: • Passivity • Navel gazing • Not putting our insights into practice • Not letting insights drive our creativity and achievement • Ignoring the needs of others	A person or group of persons gets subsumed into others when there is too *much* focus on this, which can lead to: • Abandoning the responsibility for developing our unique voice and contribution • Conforming even when it goes against what is important to us • Losing sight of who we are • Being washed away by others
Too *little* focus on this can lead to: • Neglecting our own moral compass • Neglecting our own identity	Too *little* focus on this can lead to: Losing affinity and connection with others • Permanently rebelling because we can't fit in • Never getting the support that would allow us to contribute more fully • Not allowing others to support us
Expressing Full Potential	**Service to Others**
Selfish goal striving can lead to: • Intense drive for personal success • Ruthless ambition • Frantic movement • Disregard for others • Living in a world of our own and failing to contribute our gifts	Sacrificing to others can lead to: • Martyrdom • Exhaustion • Or, as Oscar Wilde so memorably put it, 'She lives for others, you can tell them by their hunted expression'.
Too *little* focus on this can lead to: • Stifled self-expression • Failure to use and develop our unique talents • Getting others to do the challenging tasks • Inertness	Too *little* focus on this can lead to: • Inability to give • Not recognising the opportunity to contribute • Not developing the compassion to see where others need help or not knowing how to act when others need help.

Using the Map of Meaning to increase a sense of wholeness

Why is structure important to experiencing work and life as meaningful?

As we said in the first chapter, people often compare the Map of Meaning to a compass, a GPS of the inner world, a map that links us to others and yet is unique.

The structure of the Map allows us to find a way into the inner world of feelings, thoughts, beliefs and experiences. This enables us to systematically explore that inner world in relation to living and working meaningfully. The Map is not a blueprint. It does not say what we should do, but rather gives us a structure to discern where we are in relation to meaning. One person put it this way:

> I say 'Never again!' on a daily basis, but I enter a corporate setting,
> and I need to stay in touch with my feelings. I need to check, am
> I falling back into old patterns? We need to look after our humanity.
> The Map is like a template I can use to quickly check how I'm doing.

Structure, like a map, focuses attention, helps us to ask questions and look for answers in the right place. The four pathways provide a specific, yet complete, way of focusing. Rather than giving us the answers, it calls answers up out of us. 'The word structure means to build, to construct, to form . . . It can be seen as . . . a quest not only for form but also for purpose, direction and continuity' (Block 2008: 8). In the following section we explore ways to use the Map to work constructively with the tensions. We look at how we can experience a greater sense of harmony. We show that 'between the opposites lie all possibilities for growth' as Maurice Nicoll (1957: 239) says, and explore how we can learn through working with the differing needs in ourselves, because 'the quest for meaning is a quest for coherence' (Yalom 1980: 43).

Exercise 4.3

Purpose

To notice the pathways of meaning in relation to each other. To look at a part and seeing how it relates to the whole.

Instructions

- Please go back to what you have written down for Exercise 3.1. Notice, as you look at what you have written:

- When you look at each pathway, can you see how they support each other?
- Can you see how you can bring a strength developed in one pathway to another?
- What else do you notice?

One person who had spent too much time in Unity with Others began to see his conformity and questioned what fuller expression of himself could look like. Another person saw how bare Unity with Others was for her. She knew she was a loner, but for the first time saw an area of meaning that was empty and felt the sadness of it. At the same time, in identifying it through the exercise she began to see a way to address this vague depression that she had not clearly understood before, creating a greater sense of wholeness in her life.

For these people and others, there was a sense that meaningfulness had just expanded and that where they had been focused largely on one goal they now saw other areas that were important, but either underdeveloped or not noticed.

The structure of the Map allows us to examine one dimension while making sure we don't lose sight of the whole picture. This helps explain why, after having been focused on a goal of Expressing Full Potential, such as getting a qualification, and having been totally satisfied, we may suddenly notice that the savour has somehow disappeared from our studies. Using the Map quickly shows that the focus has been largely on Self and Doing, and that the next step is to examine how such a qualification could be most useful to others, or how we can reconnect with our heart space, or whether there are others with whom we might share our learning. One participant put it thus:

> The Map is like a compass, but one where you can focus on one
> quadrant and it can sort of pop out until you have finished, and
> then it can slide back down again and another one might pop up
> for you to focus on.

Working with the Map over time helps people be more aware of subtle shifts of energy in the balance of the elements, so that we can adjust more quickly and more easily. To be whole, or working towards wholeness, is to be self-healing.

In Case 4.1, one person describes how she has used the Map in her work as a Neuro Linguistic Programming coach virtually since it was created.

Case Study 4.1 **The smallest intervention**

In 2002 I had a client whose father had died six weeks before. She said her mother had been very dependent on her father, that her father was a 'slave to her mother'. The role had been transferred to her and it wasn't working for her. This wasn't the only area of her life that wasn't the way she wanted it.

As a way to clarify just what was happening I explained the Map of Meaning and asked her what percentage of her time she spent in each quadrant: '95 per cent in Service to Others and 5 per cent in expressing myself, which is all moaning about the 95 per cent in Service to Others,' she said with a grin. (I do love the way the Map can get right to the heart of the matter.)

The intervention was to task her to shift 1 per cent of her time and energy from Service to Others to developing Self and 1 per cent into Unity with Others. She took a copy of the Map home and put it on her refrigerator door.

Her mother died later that year and she told me that on the day of the funeral she noticed the Map, still on the refrigerator door, and was astonished to realise that on this significant day she was approximately 25 per cent in each quadrant.

I find as a coach, trainer and therapist that the smallest intervention that creates movement in the direction that a person wants to go in generally gets much better results than larger interventions.

This example shows that often people need to put only minimal increases into the impoverished areas to notice a marked change in how they feel. Another important point to note in this case study is that the solution enables people to identify resources that they already have in strongly developed dimensions of the Map and transfer these to less developed areas addressing an issue quickly and confidently.

The more all dimensions of meaning can be expressed the more solidly you, your colleagues, your family can stand, robust and resilient in life. This has been important for one consultant who regularly uses the Map in his work coaching individuals in organisations.

Case Study 4.2 **Using the axes of Self and Other, Being and Doing, with others**

I use the Map early on when I am coaching someone, because I want to quickly find out as much as I can about what is happening in this person's life. Especially if they are bogged down and unsure of their direction.

I just draw or highlight the two axes: Being and Doing, and Self and Others. I label them and what I've found is that people easily recognise these four terms. They certainly know Doing, Others and Self, though often Being is not very clear for them. I have found that left-hemisphere dominant people really like a graph, which is what the Map is in the way I use it.

I ask, 'Tell me where you are now'. Sometimes I suggest they put numbers on the axes, sometimes not. It depends on the interaction. I say, 'You hold the pen. You put a mark on the line which captures how much of your life is working for others? How much time in reflection, you know, mowing the lawn, biking, walking?' And I've found whatever mark they make it is usually spot on. They might say as they make the mark, 'I wouldn't know when I last had a moment to myself', so this gives me a good idea of how things are for them. Then we discuss it.

After a while, I might say, 'If you were to reduce this just a little bit, or expand this side just a little bit, what would that be like?' I have found it is really important to suggest this as a small movement, baby steps, because whatever shift they make needs to be achievable. And they are the way they are because it is in their DNA as a person, for example, to serve others. So they get a bit anxious if you suggest they focus on themselves. I say, 'Since it is in your DNA even if you really, really tried to focus just on yourself you would still find yourself helping others, so don't worry'.

Maybe after a bit more discussion, it depends on the session and the person, I might bring in Inspiration with a question like, 'What motivates you, what's your dream life?' I find out what motivates and inspires them, so we have some sense of what they want in life. Or I might pull out the Four Pathways and go through that with them. The pathways give a great description of some things we can do in each area: 'So let's look at the reality of Integrity with Self? How does it look in your real life? And how does that impact on your Inspiration, or not?'

Mostly people are totally involved in the Doing, and sometimes have trouble grasping Being. I suggested one guy stop on the way back from the coaching session and just spend fifteen minutes looking at the sea. But he couldn't do it. He came back some time later and said. 'I was biking and I came to a steep hill and I had to stop and walk for a bit, and I began to understand what you had been talking about'.

Being able to distinguish Being is so important for people, especially for managers. We need practices that force you to look at yourself, the spirit of yourself. It is often growing the Being that we need to focus on. And the Map exposes a lack of Being; a lack of self-nourishment, and self-affirmation, neglect of ourselves, and highlights this as an area for growth.

What results have I seen? I would have to say that everyone has grown in themselves, got a better sense of self, and when they have applied for promotions, they have got them. They recognise when they are out of balance and they have some strategies to deal with this. They say things like, 'It helped me understand myself so much better. I do now take time for me, and it hasn't caused me to do anything less for others'. It reframes their language and they start to speak from all aspects of the Map, so when one client was thinking of doing a PhD and I questioned it, he replied, 'It's part of increasing my Integrity with Self as well as Expressing My Full Potential'.

Creating inner order: peace and consistency

Being able to see the whole gives us clarity. There is something about seeing the whole that is restful. We are not rushing around in an overwhelming complexity searching for answers, but looking at a totality and for our answers within it. With the Map, a sense of internal integration can happen quickly, and intuitively as in this story from Jan Lagas, an early participant in one of our workshops, in Case study 4.3.

Case Study 4.3 **My journey with the map**

It happened in 2005! I was invited to participate in a weekend workshop with the Map. I was aware of lots of spiritual influences active in my life. I was not conscious of which one belonged to what. My mind was chaotic in that respect. I had read about the Map but never experienced it.

To begin with we moved from Integrity with Self to Unity with Others and during the workshops the things I learned landed. I was Being!

I became aware of the existing spirituality from the world itself. It is part of us, rooted in our very souls. The conscious thought emerged that all of us humans are capable of experiencing sadness at what is happening in the world. How we are all related and connected to this world and the universe in an organic way. All of this connects us all together. The question still is, how do we realise it?

In the next section I was pulled into the world of Service to Others and Expressing Full Potential. In the end I realised it is all available in myself. I was Doing!

I am a religious person and I believe in my Maker. This weekend made me understand that we need a balance between the source of our origin and this world, our temporal place to be for approximately 80 years. We have to learn to embrace our imperfections and not lose sight of our inspiration.

Wow, what an insight! The chaos subsided, the sky in my mind is clear and I know what I want to do more than ever before. At the end of the weekend we all had to physically express what we had gained. I literally made a mathematically precise dance, to show to myself and others, how everything was organically connected; the chaos was over.

Working with the Map over time and seeing all parts in relation to each other brings about an inner order, and this is echoed by others who have worked with the Map for years.

> I did say to people that I was experiencing a sense of inner order, but it wasn't until someone else said that they experienced it too that I began to take it seriously and wonder why this is. The Map says these are the pathways to meaning human beings have for their lives. I began to order myself around them. Over time that ordering has proved to be sound. The pathways hold, as does the rest of the structure of the Map. I find myself responding from the order of the Map, with a quietness and more confidence. This inner order occurs from simply having the Map as a frame of reference. It works on me, rather than I have to work with it.

If we are able to see and work with the four pathways, all together, all at the same time, it helps us develop more consistency in ourselves. Schumacher (1978) would refer to this as 'putting our inner house in order'. This is echoed in a comment from a participant: 'I now have the means to cease being at war with myself. It is extraordinary'. Another put it thus: 'The Map creates a harmonious relationship between you and life'.

Acting from wholeness

With the Map as a frame of reference we can draw on and develop our skills. In the following case study, we can see how this happens when an employee is introduced to the Map of Meaning.

> I had to make a decision whether to leave my job or stay. There were rumblings of redundancies and I knew that the research division was not a high priority. I love research, I love my job, but I wanted to choose. When I was introduced to the Map I knew this was what I had been looking for. I took it back to work and worked through it. I realised that few people in the organisation knew what research can offer them, so I decided that we needed to do a road-show to share this with them. This was Service to Others. I could share my love of research and my skills with them [Expressing Full Potential].

> My boss agreed, but I was faced with my shyness, so I had to develop some courage [Integrity with Self] which I did. It was very successful, and now we have lots of work. I also met so many wonderful people, and now I have lunch with different people many days a week [Unity with Others]. I have been so happy since I did this, and people around me have noticed it. The Map gave me a framework to solve my problem, grow and develop, and share my skills with my colleagues. And I know that if there are redundancies in the future I will be much more creative and therefore resilient.

This is an example of job-crafting, showing how inner wholeness gives people confidence, personal power and the force to do what they see needs to be done. And, for many, they find that when they bring this strength to the organisation, they have more freedom to recraft their jobs than they thought they did. They also find, as in the case above, that because they speak from purpose, their ideas are more easily adopted by their superiors or colleagues.

Listening from our whole selves to the whole other

One of the first things we noticed in working with the Map was how it began to shift the way people listened to each other. They began to listen to others with all the pathways to meaning in view. For example, listening to someone talking about what they might need to be creative, we would also listen to what their creativity might contribute to a wider group, or with whom they could work to give fuller expression to their creativity, or where they would need to take some contemplative time to fuel creativity, and people were able to ask more fruitful questions as a result.

Over time, we also found that staying aware of the Map as others talk can help us to see a fuller person than we might have seen before. For example, working with young prison inmates, altered how one of us was able to relate to them because it kept their human need to contribute in front of mind, even though, as teenagers in prison, this aspect of them might have otherwise been invisible to us – and to them. Acting as if 'making a difference' was something they 'naturally' wanted to do opened up very moving conversations about their longing to make a difference for their children.

Not only is it possible to listen to others from wholeness, but one consultant also describes how he used the Map to speak from wholeness, and to the wholeness in others.

Case Study 4.4 **Speaking from and to the whole person**

The indigenous people of New Zealand, the Maori, have a different view of the world from many Pakeha (the non-Maori people in New Zealand). As with many indigenous cultures, it is a view that is typically systemic and holistic. As a Pakeha working with a Maori group whose role is to provide a bridge between an essentially Pakeha system (a hospital) and the Maori users of the system, I really need to be able to understand and 'live into' this world-view.

When running a workshop with them recently I used the Map as a way of introducing myself. I knew that I had to put more focus on Unity with Others. I couldn't ignore that they were Maori and relate to them as if they were Pakeha. So I had to openly and explicitly build unity with them and let them build unity with me, because relationships are so important within Maori culture.

Bearing this in mind I said, 'Ki te Ao Marama toku marae' – 'Ao Marama (the name meaning "into the light" that we have given our house) is our spiritual home'. Then, in terms of expressing my full potential and being of service I went on to say 'Ki Te Ao Marama toku mahi' – 'Bringing things into the light, or throwing new light on things, is my work'. There was an immediate sense of rapport and understanding in the room.

Because I had come at it from the dimensions of the Map, their experience was that their *mana* (dignity, pride and more) had been respected. Combining the Map and *tikanga* Maori (the Maori way of doing things) made it even more powerful. I had moved towards them using correct language and protocol, but I also had a way of representing and expressing my fuller self. I now realise that I had been in the Integrity with Self quadrant during this entire experience; I had never spoken this way before! Using the Map (I've got to the point where I cannot avoid using it) lets me operate as big me, rather than little me, as my biggest self, rather than my limited self. It gives me a language and a structure to do that and use it to also connect with the bigger them, their bigger selves.

This case study highlights the importance of having a holistic framework as something at the back of our mind that we can speak from, especially when working with cultures who naturally have this world view. Skolimowski (1994) points out that 'wholeness is not only a descriptive term showing how parts are united within a pattern. It is also an epistemological term. Wholeness and holistic thinking are modes of understanding'. We will refer to the importance of this again in later chapters. Having a structure, a map, helps us to understand where we are and therefore to make informed and conscious choices to do with meaningfulness.

Part of living a meaningful life is that we address all pathways to meaning, and we have found the structure of the Map is very useful in designing projects involving human activities/beings. In Case study 4.5, one of us used the four pathways of the Map to support a group to create a group contract.

Case Study 4.5 **Creating a meaningful team contract**

A group of culturally very diverse students had to decide how they wanted to work with each other in order to achieve a difficult result. They had been discussing some general principles, such as 'meeting deadlines' and 'listening to each other', but it seemed to the lecturer that they were not getting to the heart of the matter. He put the Map in the middle and said: why don't you each go around the Map and tell the others what is really important to you and what that means for your teamwork? Students immediately started to engage, coming up with real examples of past group work and clearly stating what would ideally meet their expectations. For example, in 'Unity' a student said 'What I really hate is when we agree on something in the group and then a couple go away and change the agreement'. So, the group agreed that any changes to the plan would need to be put on their Facebook page with a brief explanation so all could agree. Another student in 'Expressing Full Potential' said, 'I usually go very quiet when others do not hear my idea or respond positively to it'. So, the group decided they would always list all ideas before deciding which ones to use. Another said, 'To be honest, my experience with group work is that either someone takes over, or we do a mediocre job; I want us to do a good job and I want us to do it together'. So, they agreed to set some criteria of what was a 'good job' and to hold each other to account.

In using the Map in this way, they designed a group contract that was real, whole and with which they could all identify. The lecturer later said, 'students usually never refer to group contracts again, but because this one was both simple and comprehensive, and the students really discussed what was meaningful to them, they used it all the time'.

Some research-based practices for individuals creating wholeness in their working lives

Even with little task discretion, it may still be possible to consciously bring the whole of meaningful work to it by changing the cognitive task boundaries

(Wriesnewski and Dutton 2001). For example, an academic can experience and create a consciously meaningful marking experience by balancing Self/Doing (adding unique expertise to the student paper); Other/Doing (helping the student to improve the paper); Other/Being (marking which strengthens rather than diminishes the student-academic relationship) and Self/Being (getting the ego out of the way).

When there is more discretion and organisational support, individual tasks or jobs can be designed to enhance experiences of meaning. For example, Grant (2007) found that a job was experienced as more meaningful when the individual not only made a difference, but also perceived they made a difference due to greater relational contact with those who benefit (balancing Doing/Other and Being/Other). He suggests jobs need to be designed for regular contact with beneficiaries. When a person has even greater control, they can (re-)craft their jobs (Wriesnewski and Dutton 2001) by changing the social environment of the job. For example, Bailey and Madden (2015,) found that refuse collectors experienced more meaning because they were 'able to control the pace and timing of their own work, free from managerial controls, particularly in relation to the routes chosen to collect waste'. This gave refuse collectors a sense of meaningful work because, while they already experienced 'serving others' (doing/others), they now also experienced a sense of accomplishment (doing/self): 'I was working out where I've got to be and in what order and it worked first time'. With regard to self/being Lips-Wiersma (2006) in research on organisational retreats, found that where employees were given time within working hours to, in a structured manner, reflect on what was meaningful to them (rather than consider organisational goals), this reflection opportunity resulted in participants re-crafting aspects of their work to make these more meaningful. What was particularly interesting to note in this study was that individual workers had had the freedom to re-craft their work all along. However, it was not until they had structured time to think and feel what mattered to them that they re-crafted aspects of their roles.

Examples such as these show that making the 'being' dimension visible against the background of the accelerating pace of work and life is particularly helpful. Meaningful work involves a commitment to occupy time attentively. The ability to reflect, or dialogue, allows one to invest something with significance (Parkins 2004). Noonan (2009) found that individuals balanced 'Expressing Full Potential' with 'Integrity with Self' when they were able to reflect upon and decide between different possibilities for action based on what is the right thing to do, and what feelings different causes of action evoked (e.g. anxiety, openness) (Noonan 2009). When an individual cannot express all dimensions within one job, a dynamic view of meaningful work can help to decide on the next career step to balance unmitigated dimensions of meaning (economic circumstances permitting). For example, a CEO who after years of self/doing in a commercial company moves towards other/doing in heading a charity (Tams and Marshall 2011).

In seeing the whole of meaningful work and meaningful life, an individual who cannot balance all dimensions of meaning at work can more consciously decide to balance meanings across work and life. Kofodimos (1993), in this context, addresses the agency theme of mastery, and the communion theme of intimacy. Her research shows that managers (including women) who approach work from a mastery (self/doing) perspective alone, tend not to use the intimacy-oriented approach at home. The consequences of striving for mastery and avoiding intimacy, she found, were that one experiences life as mundane and interaction with others, including spouse and children, becomes exclusively task oriented. Kofodimos (1993: 75) argues that preoccupation with one dimension of meaning at the expense of another often 'dovetails nicely with the organisation's interest in bending us to its own ends. Specifically, organisations' hierarchical structures and the very notion of advancement play on our unconscious belief that success and promotion will allow us to approach that idealised image for which we strive'. Other unmitigated expressions of meaning such as Service to Others can also be encouraged by organisations, and in Chapter 8 we will return to how the whole of the organisation needs to be designed to encourage balanced meaning. When the whole of meaning is taken into account, this can also enable individuals to consciously decide to balance the four dimensions across different life roles.

Summary

- Meaningful work is a multidimensional construct. In other words, when individuals say 'my work is meaningful because . . .' they describe several experiences of meaningful work such as belonging, moral discernment, having a sense of achievement, high-quality relationships or making a difference. As the quotes at the start of this chapter indicate, these dimensions do not evolve separate from each other, nor is meaning a static concept. It is not a recipe, nor a list, but a dynamic living response to inevitable tensions brought on by the circumstances of one's work and life.

- The different dimensions of work strengthen each other and thus the more dimensions that can be expressed at once in a task, a job or across work, family and community roles, the better we become at living meaningfully, and the more meaning we experience in our lives.

- The Map provides a simple structure so that the inevitable tensions of life and work, can be directly addressed. In addition, the Map, its axis and arrows, depict that tensions are a normal part of living, and this supports talking about lack of balance in ways that do not make anybody wrong.

- When meaning is treated as a list of things to do, it is oversimplified. When meaning is treated as overly complex, we can become discouraged and ignore it. The Map, with its simple yet profound structure, allows individuals, groups and organisations to take clear action to balance and integrate the different dimensions of meaning.

5

Taking responsibility between Inspiration and Reality

When we can give words to what is meaningful (Chapter 3) and find ways to attend to balance and increase integration (Chapter 4), our inherent capacity to live meaningfully starts to flow more naturally and with greater purpose. In this chapter we focus on the next step, which is to stay responsible for living meaningfully between Inspiration and Reality.

There is a strong link between our ability to be responsible and our ability to live meaningfully: 'In a word, each man is questioned by life; and he can only answer to life by answering for his own life; to life he can only respond by being responsible' (Frankl 1963: 72). Being responsible is not a one-off decision or a fixed identity: 'Every situation is new and demands a response that cannot be prepared beforehand. It demands nothing of what is past. It demands presence, responsibility; it demands you' (Buber 1970: 145).

It is difficult to feel inspired for long periods of time and it is often hard to continue to act on inspiration in the face of our shortcomings, the confronting circumstances of our working and personal lives, as well as the troubles facing humanity. There are many factors distracting us from living meaningfully and this too is a natural part of our search for meaning. Well-known author and social activist, bell hooks, writes about how we, as humans, are not always skilled at coming home to ourselves, and are in fact quite capable of routinely getting lost:

> Again and again as I travel around I am stunned by how many citizens in our nation feel lost, feel bereft of a sense of direction, feel as though they cannot see where our journeys lead, that they cannot know where they are going. Even the old, the elders, who have lived from decade to decade and beyond, say 'life is different in this time "way strange"', that our world today is a world of 'too much'—that this too muchness creates a wilderness of spirit, the everyday anguish that shapes the habits of being for those who are lost, wandering, searching.
>
> hooks 2009: 1

There are dangers in what bell hooks refers to as 'the habits of lostness'. Habits are what we fall back on if we do not consciously take charge of meaning, swaying between feelings of lostness and grabbing the first thing that promises to relieve that 'lost' feeling.

If we do not proactively create meaning in our communities, relationships, or working lives we are condemned to states of boredom, discontent, impotence and existential frustration and withdraw from our responsibilities to ourselves and others (Frankl 1963).

Yet if anyone were to ask us, 'Do you think it is important that you take responsibility for your own well-being and that of others?', our reply would be 'Of course'. As human beings we know the importance of taking responsibility.

> The fate of the world hangs on the thread of our individual and collective consciousness. We may wrestle at times with the inflation and deflation that accompany such a responsibility, but to deny responsibility is to take flight from what the world asks of us.
>
> Briskin 1998: 268

Briskin here talks about the inevitable inflation and deflation (of our big balloon) of responsibility. We feel inspired, we make plans and want to do the best possible job, but others might not come on board, bureaucracy might get in the way, other demands are equally pressing and we give up. We look at the state of the world and want to make things better, but when we don't know where to start, when we don't see change fast enough, when we are confronted with the negative forces happening at the same time, we give up. We anticipate great things from a new leader or colleague but then when they make mistakes, we are quick to sweep them off their pedestal. These are examples of being inspired and then deflating, wanting to make changes but being ready to be disappointed. Yet meaningful living is, in many ways, a steady plodding away at our lives.

In the original research it became clear early on that our quest for meaningfulness could be inspired by different sources which spoke to the ultimate purpose of our life, an ideal towards which to always strive, some force outside of ourselves, a hope or vision. We called this 'Inspiration', which literally means that which breathes life into our being and doing.

At the same time meaning collapses when we are too utopian, Pollyannaish or pretend that we know where we are going when we got lost long ago. Meaning does not take place in a vacuum and we need to read ourselves as we truly are, and our situation as it truly is. We simply refer to this as 'Reality' in the outer circle of the Map. With this, we do not assume that there is one reality 'out there' which we all share, but rather that meaning needs to be grounded in reality as we experience it.

When we stay present to both Inspiration and Reality, we are more likely to act on our dreams, hopes and visions for a meaningful life for ourselves and others. As one of the research participants put it:

> Your life takes place between what inspires you and the circumstances of who you are as a person and of your environment. Be present to these, take these into account when you plan your future or evaluate your past, let these forces shape you into a responsible human being. Try not to do this by yourself but draw on inspiration and do not be disappointed when you are faced by challenges in yourself and in the world. All of this is a natural part of a richly meaningful life.

In the big theatre of our life, the Map reflects that we live between 'heaven and earth', or as Simone Weil so beautifully puts it, 'between gravity and grace'. Each day, each week, each year, there will be events, interactions, information that pull us up and that pull us down, that give us hope and that make us despair. This is part of human existence. In working with the Map we have learned that the way in which we position ourselves in relation to Inspiration and Reality significantly influences the extent to which a person takes responsibility for living meaningfully. In the next section we start by exploring the sources from which you do, or could, find your inspiration.

Inspiration

The central magnetising core of the Map of Meaning is Inspiration, that which breathes life into, stimulates, animates and lifts us up. It is a place that sustains our will and determination. It is spoken of as the place of hope, dreams, visions for the future and ideals – the field of possibilities. Each of these has been fully written about, and they focus us on that which transcends our immediate experience. For example:

> It [hope] transcends the world that is immediately experienced and is anchored somewhere beyond its horizons. Hope in this deep sense is not the same as joy that things are going well, or the willingness to invest in enterprises that are obviously headed for early success, but rather the ability to work for something because it is good, not just because its stands a chance to succeed. Hope is definitely not the same thing as optimism. It is not the conviction that something will turn out well, but the certainty that something makes sense, regardless of how it turns out. It is hope, above all, which gives us the strength to live and continually try new things.
>
> Vaclav Havel 2004

Inspiration is part of our humanness and we are surrounded with examples of the importance of inspiration in our lives through myths, fairy tales, books, the lives of inspiring people, as well as inspirational art and music. They are all examples of the human drive to aspire, to take oneself on a journey towards a transcendent goal. A 'sense of meaning involves some sort of quest' (Cottingham 2003: 33). If these aspirations are dismissed there is little hope of bettering the condition of ourselves, humanity and the planet.

The Map puts Inspiration at the centre, at the heart of our experience because it is the spark that ignites and nourishes our life or the core around which life is centred. It breathes life into the various pathways of meaning and pulls us towards them. Again, 'Inspiration' may or may not be a helpful word to draw out the essence of what this element of the Map is about for you. As we saw in Japan, it also does not work in all cultures and people here preferred 'hope'.

Over the years we have heard practitioners using many questions to get to the heart of Inspiration – for example, 'What is your well-spring?', which could lead to interesting questions about what causes it to flow freely and what dams it up. Another practitioner directs people to 'look for where you replenish'. Working with the Map we can ask: what myth is guiding my life? What is life all about? What quest is my soul embarked upon? What destiny am I fulfilling? What makes me believe there is hope for the world? These questions enable people to quickly distinguish between what they think *should* drive their lives and what is truly going on.

Through Exercise 5.1 we invite you to examine your own relationship to this element of the Map.

Exercise 5.1

Purpose

To explore the source of your Inspiration.

Instructions

- Take a copy of the Map and look at the central circle.
- Ask yourself, what inspires you? (or use any of the questions above that work for you).
- Write your answer in the centre and just see how it sits with you. You may wish to try out numerous words or phrases, or just stay with one.
- Notice whether this source of inspiration is surprising to you, or something that you easily recognise.
- Notice whether it is recent or has been constant.

Over the years people have used vastly different words and experiences to describe what inspires them. Please refer to Chapter 2 for examples.

What you have written down may echo some of these examples or be entirely your own. For some people, what inspires them has been clear and certain. For others it was a surprise or a challenge to put a name to what they felt:

> In doing this exercise I realised that really I have no answer, that life is a mystery, and so, somehow, what is at the heart of everything for me is a Great Mystery. What was important for me was that, for the first time, I was naming this, saying it, beginning to wonder, 'Well, if it's all so mysterious, how does that guide my life?'

One person commented, rather anxiously, that she had put 'anger' into the centre, 'because it is my anger and rage at what's going on that inspires me, is that all right?' We suggested she stay with what she had put down, and she went on to examine more fully this aspect of herself. Many people are inspired by 'righting wrongs', and others by their family or aspects of their work.

In doing or facilitating this exercise, it may be useful to ask more questions to learn more about the meaning of the word we place in the centre: for example, What is it about family, nature, the next generation, or God that inspires you? It might draw out words that are simultaneously more precise and more universal. Or, in the case with the person who put anger in the centre, it could be useful to ask, what is it that is outraged? What fundamental commitment is negated in the issues that make you angry? Depending on the initial question you asked, you can continue along the same theme. For example, if you asked yourself, what replenishes me? You can also ask how empty or how full you are, what drains and what fills up your heart.

We have found that, if time and space permit, it can be helpful to send people outside into nature or, if this is not possible, to use techniques (visioning, meditation) or materials (art, poetry) to help people go deeper.

What is at the centre is permanent for some people while for others it changes as they make shifts within themselves. It is important to stress that both are OK. The key question in doing this exercise is whether what is put at the centre is still very much alive. For example, one person reflected:

> At times I am trying to get closer to God and do God's bidding, so obviously God is at the centre. But at the moment that is not the case at all. The word 'God' does not really bring things alive for me at present; it is an automatic response but now seems too abstract. I need something more tangible.

Some people put down something very practical, such as 'success' or 'financial security', because many people have a very goal-oriented way of thinking about themselves and their lives. Asking more questions may help them see what lies behind these goals. For example, one person put 'success in my career' in the centre and then explored this through the four pathways to see whether this particular goal actually continued to be a real source of Inspiration. Once he had tested it through the four pathways by asking, what does my career serve? How does my career create unity?, etc. he arrived at: 'to keep my working life vibrant and apply it to worthwhile outcomes' as his source of Inspiration. We learned to work with what people put in the centre even when we might, at least initially, judge it as a limited goal rather than a transcendent vision. A certified practitioner relates the following story of working with inspiration:

> I had a client who put 'money' in the centre. I was surprised, and questioned her about this. However, she remained firm that for her money was at the centre. I became interested in why money was so important to her. She then reflected on the pathways in the Map and reeled off the huge number of things she wanted to do with money (with others, for others, who she could become if she had money), which made me see things quite differently.

In such situations, bringing in the other elements of the Map of Meaning, the four pathways and also the tensions, provides the person with tools to get more concrete, to understand the 'why' behind the 'how' and thus, in this case, to understand their commitment to this goal by breaking the big question into smaller parts and then returning to the bigger questions of 'What is behind it all for me?' or 'What drives it all for me?'

People draw on different inspirations at different times or in different contexts. We know of many people who keep their own version of the Map of Meaning on an office wall and check in with it during the day. For them it is also important to know that the words are still alive. When you use the Map for a longer period of time it is important to continue to question: Does this still hold true for me? Is this still life-giving, uplifting, vibrant? Asking questions like these is part of taking responsibility.

It can also be helpful to make a connection between the source of Inspiration and a specific aspect of work, such as leadership, innovation, meetings or client interactions, or to a specific aspect of family life. Again it is important to ask: and if you put this (the source of Inspiration) at the heart of your leadership/fatherhood what difference would it make for you? For others? And so test this focus through the pathways to see if it remains meaningful, and also to gain practical insight into how the vision can be expressed.

If people are unsure about what is in the centre for them other questions might be helpful; Where *might* I/you get my Inspiration? How much Inspiration am I accessing? Where is it naturally present, where do I need to make an effort? One participant said:

> It shows us when the centre is weak and may not be providing enough inspiration because the Map is like a gyroscope. The wobbliness of the edges—if you look at it as a 3-D map—makes it so important that we take time to really contact what inspires us at the core. You can see why it is so important to have a strong core. It helps us to weather the storms.

Sometimes people have no immediate response to what is at the heart of things for them. It is important to allow them to take the time they need to work with this.

> When the Map was up on the board my attention was grabbed by the centre of the Map staring at me like a target on a dartboard. I found myself beginning a search not only for the missing words in that target but also for my own spirituality, something that I would have assured you was never part of my work. On the Map that was used in my workshop this inner circle is a sun-like shape. For me this shape represents and looks like 'the light at the end of the tunnel', which gave me a huge sense of possibility and a small

> affirmation that I was making discoveries already. At this point the
> word was most definitely 'hope'.

Sometimes reality is so challenging that Inspiration can seem too much to ask of ourselves. A person with a chronic illness said, 'I can't afford to have inspiration. It exhausts me to even think about it'. What worked was to acknowledge that this was how it was for him, and then ask, 'Can you take a step, however small, in each pathway?', which he could. Interestingly, many years later, this person had set small goals and accomplished them and credited the Map as giving him a way to keep both his reality and his desire for a better life in focus, in a way he could manage. It also happens that people have one of the quadrants in the centre. Often it is Service to Others. Our observation is that this points to an area of potential imbalance. Again it is important to not invalidate it in any way, but to explore it with skilful questions, if that is appropriate.

In the same way that we talked about 'balance and wholeness' in the previous chapter, it is important to create the right relationship between inspiration and reality. Inspiration can be overwhelming and once, when doing this exercise, a person got really upset. 'Actually, I am sick of Inspiration! I have been so inspired and all it has done it turn people off!' Since we were doing the exercise with the Map on the floor, the facilitator just picked up Inspiration and said, 'Great. This is your Map, you can have it just the way you want. Where do you want me to put Inspiration?' 'Out there, under a book, with just a bit showing that is fine'. In the meantime, the participant had picked up Integrity with Self and was clutching it to her heart. 'Well, Integrity with Self seems important to you?', the facilitator asked. To which the participant laughed and said, 'Yes, I can see that it is'.

With regard to balance and wholeness, the Map is also of real value to people who are naturally driven by Inspiration. Many highly creative people, budding entrepreneurs or youth have great challenges in being with reality in a constructive way. They have been told to 'get real' so many times that they disconnect inspiration from reality and either just push on or become overly ambitious. In this case it can be very useful to ask, 'what is the smallest step you can take towards making this real?' In one situation, where a person was committed to a massive social transformation, inspiration burned so brightly that it was exhausting even though he had accomplished a great deal. He realised that he needed to consolidate, bring others on board and develop new skill levels.

One example of insight that arose from working with the Map between inspiration and reality can be found in the following story of deliberately integrating the two dimensions of the Map.

> I have a huge vision. And I am a person who has definitely had trouble grounding my visions at times, although I have been working at it over the years. Working with the Map one day I stood in my office and faced up to the fact that the gap between my Inspiration and Reality was huge. I often swung between the two, which meant that I was either pushing things, or collapsed and procrastinating. I put one arm up in the air to signal inspiration, and the other down low to signal reality and then slowly I brought them together. Staying in this position for a while I said to myself, 'This is what intention feels like, when inspiration and reality are together, so that reality is fully present in my visionary moments and the vision is fully present when I am facing challenges'. It brought such a calmness to me, a certainty that my vision would be realised and that all I needed to do was keep going. I have kept that calmness, well most of the time, and it stopped me from getting too excited, or too depressed. It removed a lot of the volatility from my work, and brought a persistent, calm productivity to it instead.

In *The Fifth Discipline*, Peter Senge (1997) writes that many adults have little sense of what truly inspires them. He writes that it is important to distinguish our immediate goals and objectives from the bigger vision or inspiration that is behind them so that we can remain open to the many ways in which that vision can be achieved. Peter Block (2003), in *The Answer to How is Yes*, explains that whereas goals focus on how to get somewhere, it is the 'why' questions that connect our whole being to the deeper purpose behind the goal.

At the same time, there is the seductive power of Inspiration. Charismatic leaders create a vision that transcends reality: sometimes for good, sometimes to the harm of those who follow them. In organisational context we will come back to this in Chapter 6, but it is useful to see through the Map, our own inclination to be seduced by visions – or our resistance to them.

Reality of Self

In working with meaning, we find that the minute we aspire to something, the Reality of our Selves, including our abilities and also our limitations, simply pops up. When we are inspired, we also need to learn to notice our personal response to the dynamic dance between Inspiration and Reality.

For example, one person noticed that she is a natural enthusiast. She can always see possibility in situations and relies on enthusiasm to keep her going.

Of course, enthusiasm waxes and wanes, and she saw she gives up when the first wave of enthusiasm hits the challenges of Reality. Seeing this was helpful to her because it allowed her to look at what other qualities she needed in order to keep going with a project once the initial Inspiration had faded, and to sometimes be a little more wary of the ease with which she became inspired. It also helped her to enlist assistance earlier in the real difficulties that the project faced.

It might be helpful to do another exercise that enables you or those you work with to better understand the Inspiration–Reality dynamic.

Exercise 5.2

Purpose

To see your relationship with the Reality of your Self.

Instructions

- Take a piece of paper and write down something that inspires you or that is a source of inspiration to you.

- Now think what you have done with this inspiration to make it into a reality.

- After a short time, shift your focus to how you now feel and examine for a moment how you relate to your accomplishment to this point.

- Did you write down the small things you have already achieved or did you focus on the things you have not yet accomplished?

- How do you feel about yourself?

- What else do you observe?

In doing Exercise 5.2 you may become aware that over time you have a certain way of relating to the Reality of your Self. It can be particularly illuminating to see how you talk to yourself. Somewhere between 'this is just who I am, it will have to be good enough' and 'of course I can always improve myself, hold the possibility for a better me' is where a lot of our self-conversation take place. As one person said:

> I found it so helpful to do this exercise because I can now see how wildly I've been swinging between 'I'm great, I can do anything I put my mind to' and 'I'm small, what difference can I make?'. In working with this part of the Map I can now see that they are both true and that with that knowledge I can move steadily closer to what I'm trying to achieve.

People have very different responses when they face up to the Reality of Self. For some, the wise course is to decide what to work on: for example, trust or patience or inclusiveness. Some people make sudden changes as the result of a powerful insight. Yet for others it was simply permission-giving: 'so I am not perfect; well, I'm no longer going to wait for the perfect self to emerge, I'm just going to get on with it anyway'. For all of us there are times when the 'reality' of who we are may simply fall short of who we hoped we had become. Facing this became, for some participants, central to being more tolerant with the imperfections of other people as well as of themselves. Whatever insights we may gain, the Map can help us work with our personal patterns and also help us to plan for those unavoidable times when we lose touch with our Inspiration.

What we have also found in working with this aspect of the Map is that there is a lot of laughter. Sharing our humanity as we stare the reality of ourselves in the face helps us stop obsessing and instead find things (and ourselves) funny. Humour can provide the release of tension in the rediscovery of common sense and common humanity.

It is important to find language that makes the losing and finding of inspiration neither right nor wrong. It is, after all, just part of the reality of being human, of being ourselves. Some people could acknowledge to themselves for the first time that they were no longer inspired, that the energy was sucked out of their work or lives because they no longer felt any Inspiration. It is hard to say 'I'm a teacher but I don't really care', or 'I'm a consultant and I get paid well for making very little difference' or 'I'm a mum, but I often find myself doing things out of duty rather than love'. It is really important to recognise the courage that making such statements requires.

At a recent presentation of the Map, two nurses disclosed that they were no longer at all inspired by their work and asked, 'But what are we to do? It's good money and we're both living on our own. We need to keep going as long as we can. We can't afford to notice that we no longer like our work'.

As facilitators we sometimes feel tempted to suggest 'solutions', but work-ing with the Map helps us to support people to create their own meanings. As the facilitator who worked with the nurses said:

> In the past, if two people came to me and said 'we've talked about inspiration in our work and actually feel we don't really care about it anymore', I would have probably tried to fix it. But through working with the Map I could just go, 'yes, that is good to notice', knowing that on the way home they would chat together about this in the car and use the Map to make some conscious decisions about it.

Of course, lack of Inspiration can become contagious and otherwise become a problem for an organisation and we'll come back to this in Chapter 6.

Reality of Circumstances

The Reality of our Self is, of course, not separate from the Reality of our Circumstances. And while it is true that we all look at the world through different eyes and have different responses to it, it is important to see our circumstances as outside us. In this way we can distinguish our responsibility in light of those circumstances. For one person the reality of her circumstances really hit her when she looked at what inspired her: 'I like to think that I do this work to help people see the possibilities of life even when they are often very sick, but in reality I am not working from that energy, I am stuck in paperwork and meetings'. The important point here is that the person can see their inspiration in relation to their current reality. This way they can make choices, either to re-craft their job, address issues with a manager, find a different job or find new ways of working from the original inspired energy, or find something outside of work that inspires. Accepting an uninspired way of working can happen slowly and become a habit. It affects everyone around us – colleagues, clients, bosses and most likely our family and friends.

In this section we explore a range of responses people have to the Reality of their Circumstances. But we will begin with Exercise 5.3 for you to explore your own response to the Reality of your Circumstances.

Exercise 5.3

Purpose

To explore the impact of circumstances on your Inspiration.

Instructions

- Looking back at Exercises 5.1 and 5.2, notice how your circumstances play a part in whether or not you are able to maintain connection with your Inspiration.

- Make sure that you carefully note all circumstances that affect your situation. Try not to self-censure at this point, e.g. don't go 'oh, that is not really a big deal'; just write it all down.

- Is there one specific circumstance that challenges you, or does it 'all just seem too hard'?
- What ways do you have to support yourself in keeping going?
- What continues to defeat you?

The first thing that we often notice when we ask people to describe their 'circumstances' is that some self-editing takes place. 'Surely, this is only a small thing, others have it much worse.' For example, we originally wrote this book during the major earthquakes in Christchurch, New Zealand. We noticed how people found it hard to accept their grief about broken family heirlooms, because 'others have lost everything'. Of course it is good to see things in perspective, but it is also good to accept what you feel and how that might result in a loss of meaning. Heirlooms might be precious because they connect you to your family.

It is difficult to understand our responses to circumstances if our real feelings are not properly acknowledged. We noticed how, when we asked people to describe their circumstances at work, it was often the first time that they gave themselves permission to consider how some of these had actually stripped away a lot of meaning from their lives. It also helps many people see these circumstances clearly separate from themselves. The question then usually shifts from 'why do I feel so uninspired at work?' to 'what can I do to meet my needs for meaning, *within* this work context?'

Another thing we noticed is that facing circumstances can release enormous energy. For example, after the earthquake, we heard of a man who, overnight, became an inspired builder of outside toilets. Another man humorously and successfully auctioned for charity a boulder that had gone through his house. One woman immediately started to collect aid in her own town, drove overnight to the city, identified the poorest suburb and went to work knocking on elderly people's doors, finding many without food, water or power, some still cowering under beds and tables. This woman watched the same news as so many did that night, and many others have the skills she has, but she allowed the circumstances to enter her heart and responded because she felt 'there really was no other choice'.

In facing your circumstances, you may notice that you have become resigned, even despairing about things and feel overwhelmed or lost in some way. At times, you may have decided that this is as good as it is going to get and, at least for the time being, meaning will need to come from other roles. Or you may see that over the years you have become more robust and resilient and have some good coping strategies. You may find your current circumstances quite exhilarating and feel things have never been better. You may notice how circumstances such as health, a boss, a relationship (or lack of it), family circumstances or even the evening news can impact on how you feel. We all have different ways of making sense of our circumstances. One person talks about 'allowing the ebb and flow of life' as a way of being with the events that life brings; another says, 'The universe keeps bringing us the same lessons, until we learn them'. Circumstances can crush people and be too brutal and overwhelming. Reality can be the graveyard of dreams, aspirations, longing and hope. And reality can be a place of inner development. It can strip us to the bone, reshape and purify us in some way, making us humble, strong and compassionate. Some are inspired by circumstances; they are the making of these people. For example, students who set up or became part of the student-volunteer army during the Christchurch earthquakes. Each of us responds to circumstances in our own way.

In Case study 5.1 we see how once we can objectively work with our circumstances we can more easily reconnect with what inspires us – even when the circumstances remain largely the same.

Case Study 5.1 **Finding Inspiration in Reality**

I had been telling the same story about my workplace for a while. I would have conversations with others at work about the bad decision-making and how it sucked the energy from me. Of course, I would pick my battles and challenge some of this, but overall, work was increasingly draining my energy. One evening I was talking to a friend who works with the Map. She asked me to list all the things in my work circumstances that depleted my life-force. I arrived at the following list:

- I spend less time with the children and more with the parents.
- Because of new safety regulations the extra-curricular activities that I would enjoy and volunteer for, such as tramping, have been cut.
- We have gone to a new roster, which means my breaks always coincide with minding children in the playground.
- Meeting times have moved to after school times, often conflicting with the needs of my own young family.

What I noticed was that the list was pretty big. What I also noticed was that all of these things were true; I had not written down anything that was not real.

Contrary to my expectations, facing my 'list of woes' did not make me feel depressed. It made me realise how many distractions there were to what I inherently love to do: teach the children. It also made me realise that in each of the elements of the Map there were circumstances that made it harder to experience those rich meanings. For example, in Unity with Others, I no longer got to spend as much time with fellow teachers and parents during the tramps; in Self and Other I had hardly any time to myself during the day because of the way the breaks were now scheduled and I already have a job that is very Other-oriented. In Expressing Full Potential I had been letting go of professional development opportunities because they just seemed another thing on my list of things to do. This exercise made me realise that I had lost many things that were meaningful to me and that my circumstances had really changed.

My first reaction was to draw up a list with things in my circumstances (or context) that I really liked. That was helpful because it allowed me to see reality as it truly was, with all the positive things that I still liked about my job.

Now that I had mapped all circumstances, it also raised the question, What are you going to do in response to these? I divided them up into things I did control and things I could not control. Some things that I had challenged before became clearer and so now I could put forward a clearer argument. For example, I again challenged the lunch breaks, explaining that I needed some time in the day to reflect and evaluate and that this was central to my professional well-being and the quality of my teaching. This time I was heard. We came up with a new roster that allowed me to take those breaks at least three times a week. Other issues I still could not change but I could change my position on them once I understood why they were so important to me. For example, I realised that I needed to replace the tramps with something else that included colleagues and parents and arrived at a different physical activity that included both. Some things, such as the amount of time parents took up, I could more proactively put some boundaries around in a way that the parents understood by explaining that I needed most of my energies to go to the kids. Some things I could make more conscious choices about, such as picking one professional development activity that felt light or fun or energising. Some things, such as the meeting times, I couldn't change and it clarified that I needed to draw on additional help at home for a few hours a week.

Doing this exercise helped me to do three things:

- My discontent changed from 'a feeling' to something I could clearly see and hence actively manage. I no longer felt impotent even though there were still many times when I could not change my circumstances.
- I could better place myself in relation to my circumstances. I could more clearly see 'this is what I can control and this is where I can create more meaningful

work', 'this is what I cannot control and where I can work more actively to not get lost in my circumstances, to not let them erode my love for my job'.

- I could decide better how I wanted to be with others in relation to our shared circumstances. For example, I realised that while at first it was good to talk to colleagues about things that didn't work for us, having the same conversations over and over again also felt powerless and dispiriting. I'm working at ways we can still face our shared reality but also talk to each other in ways that are encouraging and appreciative.

We will always battle with imperfection and constraints. Anselm Gruen (1999) suggests that the Latin word *humilitas* has at its root *humus*, the earth. Humility is befriending our earthly gravity, the world of our instincts, material demands or needs, and shadow sides. Humility is therefore the courage to see reality.

When we embrace our earthliness we often also get a clearer perspective on who we are and our relationship with the transcendent.

It was surprising how often the need to feel grounded arose as a core part of our conversations about meaningfulness at work:

> There is nothing wrong with all of this mission and vision and values stuff itself. However, if we are not allowed to articulate where we do not and cannot live up to this, it feels as if we mock something that is really quite profound.

Whereas many commented it was a great relief and that it was grounding to use a map (and way of working) that squarely addressed their sense that life is hard and used terms such as 'facing imperfections', some felt it needed to be positively framed, for example, as 'opportunities to learn'. But others felt this would be too prescriptive, in the sense that meaningfulness also came from having the freedom to just face what is without immediately framing possible solutions.

The overwhelming response to seeing the space between Inspiration and Reality, within the Map, has been a sense of calmness. It helps those who are visionaries see the value of realists; while the people who get anxious as visionaries speak of a world beyond their understanding, can more easily listen and ask questions from within the possibility of the vison – rather than to mock and destroy it.

In practical terms, whether in our families, communities or immediate work relationships, the Map helps visionaries to increase the solidity of their vision, and encourages realists to be more patient, persistent and supportive as they push the visionary to clarify their ideas. It connects these two polarities as both are part of our human need for meaning. Then it gives us four pathways as ways to practically begin to weave the connection between one and the other, understanding the value of all those who contribute, in all elements in the Map.

Summary

In this chapter we addressed the relationship between Inspiration and Reality at a personal level. Between Inspiration and Reality, between possibility and failure, between idea, ideal, vision and actuality, is where the human experience takes place. It is between these two aspects of our lives that we experience the challenge and essence of living, of being human. In this sense what the Map offers is a clear picture of the field of our human experience.

The presence of Inspiration *and* Reality of Self and Circumstances in the Map offers something that is very simple and very profound. The human being cries out for a way of making sense of our lives that shows we are more than our concerns, our roles or our interests. Our ability to elevate ourselves can be inspired in numerous ways and the exercises help you to get in touch with what inspires you. At the same time we are imperfect beings who function in an environment that presents numerous challenges to our ideals. The importance of making both of these present, as the Map does, is that:

- The Map is true to life as we experience it.

- We can check our own relationship with inspiration and reality and distinguish unhealthy, discouraging or paralysing ways of engaging with them as well as encouraging, vibrant and life-giving ways of taking responsibility and creating meaningful lives.

- We can take reality into account when we are taking action from inspiration so that we will not give up or be disappointed. And we know where to find the inspiration and stay responsible in spite of setbacks.

- We can bring understanding to our work with others, wherever their natural emphasis is, whether in creating new possibilities, or being grounded in the real, and see how we all try to work between these polarities. This can increase our skill in helping ourselves and others live more comfortably and fruitfully in this vast space of human experience.

In the previous three chapters we have looked at how we can give words to meaning, put different life meanings in constructive relation to each other and take responsibility for living meaningfully. In the next section we discuss the relevance of these to transforming organisational practice and design.

Part 2

Where meaning meets organisation

As we have discussed in the first part of the book, meaning is an intrinsic aspect of being human and work, where we spend a significant part of our lives, has a major impact on our ability to experience meaningfulness. Every day people go to work hoping to use their talents, energy and effort in some activity that feels meaningful to them. Sometimes they return home feeling they got a good day's work done, and other times they return home frustrated. But what can organisations do, so that people feel they have had a meaningful day at work?

Most organisations that we work in were not designed with the quest for meaning in mind. Yet, as thinking on work has changed; as human understanding of ourselves has developed; and as we face a complex, challenging future in which so much is at stake, there is a demand to rethink the purpose and design of work.

In this second part of the book, we explore:

- how the Map of Meaning supports employees, managers and leaders to rise above the immediate demands of organisational life;

- how it helps them to evaluate every plan and practice in relation to the human need for meaningful work;

- why this is important to do.

The importance of keeping our human needs in view

Recently a document was brought to our attention by one of our colleagues. It was a set of instructions for the implementation of a revised IT system. What struck our colleague was that, in handwriting, at the top of the document the CEO had written, 'Above all do not forget that the people who are to be using this system are human beings'.

In pointing out the humanity of the people using the IT system, the CEO may have intended to keep visible something that is lost daily in the workplace. When we forget our humanness in our organisational thinking and planning we dehumanise our workplaces through a cumulation of practices and policies and, therefore, unconsciously remove meaning from much of our work.

And while it is charming to hear about a CEO who points out that there are human beings at work in this organisation, how would it have been received if someone in a lower position in the organisation had raised this? How would it have been heard, and what difference would it have made, if one of the 'end-users' had pointed out that they were human beings and that what was being implemented, or how it was done, diminished their humanity in some way? How would they have voiced this in a way that it could be heard? Would it have worked for them to simply say (as people in organisations so often do) 'I don't understand the point of this change?'

A less generous interpretation of the CEO's communication might suggest he was warning the implementers that they would have to deal with human beings who might make things difficult. Do those higher up in the organisation expect human beings to get in the way? And, if so, what exactly gets in the way of what? This issue has long been documented. Henry Ford asked, 'Why do I always have to deal with the whole person when all I want is a pair of hands?' Anita Roddick noted more than a century later, 'We advertised for employees but we found that people turned up instead'. And if people are seen as a nuisance at work, then what happens to the meaning that is of such importance to us?

Organisations are paradoxical. On the one hand, they organise their practices on the assumption that what intrinsically motivates and engages employees is central to the success of the organisation. They need engaged people at work, giving their best to the organisation. On the other hand, with a relentless focus on productivity and efficiency, organisations are extremely challenging contexts in which to work and live meaningfully.

In the following chapters, we look at how to use the Map to:

- powerfully take responsibility between inspiration and reality in contemporary organisations;

- integrate policies, practices and systems to increase organisational coherence;

- support engagement of all employees in creating and maintaining meaningful work.

We show how this can be done in teams, through redesigning an organisational practice (such as performance appraisal or job design) or rethinking major aspects of organisational structure, or the design of organisations themselves. We show how having the Map at your fingertips enables you to respond practically in any situation, at any time, from the higher purposes you have for your role, your team, your organisation.

The human need for meaning is not a fad

Human needs are often referred to as 'the soft issues'. However, as we showed in earlier chapters, this language is not helpful. It would be more accurate to think of them as 'the most meaningful issues'. Lisl Klein, who did extensive research on meaningful work, writes that the consequences of ignoring these issues can often stay invisible until it is too late:

> It [labelling something as soft] is a way of avoiding their reality, as if human reactions are somehow ephemeral, intangible, impossible to confront. They are not. What is true is that human and social systems are very adaptable, can adjust to many situations and therefore do not appear to demand early attention as clearly as economic or technical or green factors demand it. The nature of the adjustments they make may then later be felt to be undesirable, without the causal links being recognized.
>
> Klein 2008: 289

It may therefore be better to think of meaning as a subtle yet very important part of the organisation. Important because the negative effects of a disengaged worker for him or herself, and for the organisation, have not only been well documented but have also been taken seriously by many organisations. A large amount of money continues to be invested in management techniques designed to speak to, and draw on, our deeper human needs and values: intrinsic motivation management, job enrichment, total quality management, organisational culture development, ethics management and vision and values management, and, of course, leadership development. More recently workplace spirituality, flourishing, positive organising and other workplace engagement techniques have been introduced. All of these are based on the fundamental recognition that it is important to bring our humanity to work, and to address a conviction held by people at all levels of the organisation that there must be a better way to organise human beings.

Yet, without a profound understanding of what drives us at the deepest level it is easy to be seduced by the latest trend, bright idea or consultant panacea, while the basics, such as consulting employees in changes affecting them, are still not addressed. This is financially costly to organisations but also breeds increasing cynicism among staff and management, because fads and techniques are often superficial and/or piecemeal and do not address the deeper issues affecting the workplace, one of which is meaning in all its complexity.

Complexity and fragmentation are so much part of organisational life and can seem so overwhelming that we can be tempted to grab a quick fix that promises respite without contemplating *why* such interventions need to occur in the first place, or without checking whether everyone has the same understanding of why change needs to occur. It also means that those who object to these interventions are often at risk of being seen as 'obstructive', 'unreal' or 'change resistant' as they struggle to articulate their concerns. In the worst case they are told they have been consulted, while they have had no meaningful input at all.

The human quest for meaning is not a fad, and will endure long after most management techniques have been and gone. Working with it takes change processes back to basics because the Map allows collective involvement into creating and protecting meaningful work from the bottom up. This means no one person or group takes over the whys and hows of change processes, as both the outcome and the process of getting there will be collectively negotiated. It also allows us to keep all aspects of human meaning in view as we design or refine organisational structures and practices and this, as Klein says, is vitally needed.

> The biggest intellectual, methodological, and eventually cultural challenge to us is to find ways of connecting the macro and the micro, the visionary and the mundane, so that it becomes

> structurally impossible to consider the one without also at the
> same time considering the other.
>
> Klein 2008: 71

The Map, because it is easily grasped, helps us all to have a way of viewing both the macro and micro at a very profound level. This helps us to examine organisational practice and to assess what is present and what is missing so that we can, both as individuals and as an organisation, influence in a way that really does make a difference and that is sustainable over time.

Simple questions are at the heart of creating meaningful work

How often do we ask: is this current practice or planned change going to make work more or less meaningful? This, and other questions, go to the heart of creating and sustaining meaningful work. These questions are not simple to answer, and it is easy to understand why, often unintentionally, the fall-back position at work is for the collective discourse (such as meetings) to treat every issue, every change, every day, as a simple set of mechanistic tasks to resolve. However, if meaningful work is ignored, made invisible or is in some way seen as inferior to an ideal of the organisation as an efficient machine, issues of meaning are easily lost. When this happens there are implications for both the individual and the organisation. People cannot be treated as parts of a machine without losing connection to themselves and each other.

Focusing on the question of how to manage the human being without asking who the human being is and what are their needs, time and again leads to turning something as profound as the human need for meaning into an empty practice, applied when it suits an organisational goal and ignored when it is more convenient to treat human beings as a tool.

Employees often speak of their frustration that the organisation uses all the 'right language' but still not does treat them as responsible human beings. Managers often speak of wanting to share responsibility, and the need for engagement, but of employees still not stepping up to the challenge. This goes to the heart of an 'us' versus 'them' impasse where it is still assumed that those lower in the organisation's hierarchy need to be motivated whereas those higher up do the motivating.

Each person knows what is meaningful and when meaning is lost

The cure to people issues at work has usually been to focus on motivational techniques. But this misses the point.

Our research shows that human beings are by their very nature motivated by meaningful work, but because this is not well understood, it is often not considered and therefore unconsciously destroyed. People do not want someone else's meaning – they have and want their own. They do not want to be 'motivated'. They want to be given conditions that allow them to remain connected to, or enable them to reconnect with, what they consider makes their work meaningful. This is one of the key insights our work offers, because the Map of Meaning allows you to clearly understand people's process of meaning-making and therefore to work with existing meaning – your own included. The Map helps everyone to easily and practically recognise, and factor in, the human need for meaningful work and plan accordingly.

We do see more and more involvement and sustainable practice in organisations that are well ahead of the pack. We live in a time in which alternatives are not just interesting ideas, but have been shown to work, and to work sustainably. Some of these organisations no longer try to motivate people but focus on creating environments that enable people to work meaningfully in their own way (Briskin 1998). Others focus on how to create environments in which people are intrinsically free and equal (Carney and Getz 2009). Yet others have found that redefining their purpose has had substantial impact on the extent to which their employees experience meaningful work (Ellsworth 2002).

Chapter overview

In the previous chapters we showed how the Map of Meaning is central to our ability to voice, be whole and take constructive responsibility between reality and inspiration. In the next three chapters we pick up each of these themes in reverse order and discuss them in the organisational context.

In Chapter 6 we explore the tension between Inspiration and Reality in which contemporary organisations find themselves. This provides a clear context for working with the Map of Meaning, so that the complexities of organisational life do not overwhelm our ability to create meaningful work.

In response to complexity, management often falls back on traditional command and control practices and structures, which creates dependency of staff on managers. We show how the Map places responsibility for working with the gap between Inspiration and Reality firmly with all members of the organisation.

In Chapter 7 we look at how to create practices and systems that are integrated and respond to the needs of the whole human being, and that encourage a unified response by staff and managers throughout the organisation.

In Chapter 8 we look at how, by collectively developing the skills to voice, create, and remove barriers to meaningful work, it is possible to shape the organisation's own solution to the question of how to keep employees engaged, letting go of the need to constantly look outside for the latest solution.

For each of these chapters we show how meaningful (and meaningless) work shapes, and is shaped by, organisational systems. As in the previous chapters, we draw on a combination of exercises, case studies, learning and insights from ourselves and others as well as the wisdom of scholars in organisation studies.

6

Taking responsibility between Inspiration and Reality in contemporary organisations

Ideally, organisations are driven by their purpose, and much energy is put into purpose and mission statements. Yet, so often the mission is left sitting on a sign on the wall, or a computer screen. It does not become a driver for the people in the organisation, the lever for change, or the standard against which actions are evaluated. What happens when there is a gap between the vision and the lived experience of the people working in the organisation?

Figure 6.1 shows that between the purpose and the systems designed to fulfil this purpose, is the human experience. Here we can explore how the systems so often frustrate people's ability to engage with and express the vision.

In this chapter we show how the Map of Meaning enables people to clearly express their experience of which systems frustrate, and which systems support, both the purpose and their experience of meaningful work. Doing this with both managers and staff in the room helps to explain why staff are not engaged, and also to create joint solutions.

At the centre of this diagram is the particular organisation's purpose or reason for existing (usually stated on their website). It is increasingly

Figure 6.1 **Outside-in versus inside-out organising (adapted from Wouter Hart, Verdraaide Organisaties 2012)**

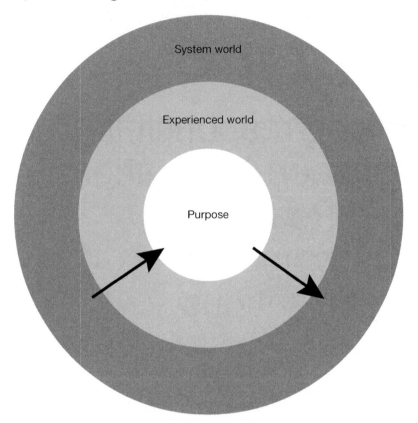

recognised that the purpose of the company itself needs to rise above the immediate reality of the organisation. Companies are therefore increasingly defining 'purpose beyond profit'. The reason for this is simple: it meets the human need for inspiration, driving sustainable success and long-term profit. Together with principles and values, purpose is what a great company stands for and would stand by even if adhering to them resulted in a competitive disadvantage, missed opportunity or increased costs (Jackson and Nelson 2004: 299). We will come back to purpose and how it can inspire all members of the organisation later in this chapter.

The outside of Figure 6.1 above depicts the systems. Much managerial energy goes into putting the systems in place to achieve the purpose. Structures, managers, teams, performance criteria, goals, outputs, are all part of this systems world. And so the organisation works from the outside to the inside. The underlying assumption is 'if we put the systems in place, our purpose will be met'. The figure above shows how this works.

The 'experienced world' circle depicts the world of experience of those working for the organisation (including managers). Here, between the systems world, and the purpose the organisation has, is the world as *experienced* by employees as they go about their daily tasks. This is the place where issues of employee motivation actually arise.

It is a world often talked about in terms of :

1 **emotions**: 'I love it when . . .', 'I get so frustrated when . . .', 'I fear . . .';

2 **energy**, and how it is intentionally or unintentionally directed: 'I'm going to . . .', 'I won't . . .', 'I can't . . .';

3 **habits**: 'that will never work because . . .' 'meetings are always . . .';

4 **power**: 'no-one thinks of asking me'; 'they asked for our input, then ignored it and did their own thing'.

While the world of experience is often expressed in emotions, energy, habits, and power (or lack of it), within this middle circle, is the natural human desire for meaningful work.

In this world of experience, inspiration and the reality of the systems in which people work either come together, in which case the individual experiences meaningful work, or they fail to connect, in which case the individual becomes despondent, angry, insecure, unsettled or starts to protect their own patch. When inspiration and reality do not come together, individuals may invest a huge amount of emotional labour in trying to find meaning, which affects not only others at work, but also family life.

The cost of speaking to inspiration OR reality, but not both

When we speak we draw the attention of others to issues and ideas of concern to us. Discourse, as Foucault says, is a power to be seized and what is 'permissible' to speak about changes, and reflects shifts in power when it does. A powerful discourse has the ability to influence our individual lives and our institutions. It has the power to shape the future. Much is at stake. Therefore it is important to think deeply and rigorously about how a new discourse is framed and voiced, and who gets involved in shaping it.

One example is the annual inspirational speech about 'the journey we are all taking in the company', and as you walk out the door you hear employees saying, 'So, where are we going?' or 'I heard he used this exact speech up north as well', or 'What has this to do with us?' or 'Well, she obviously has never worked in our department/branch/area of the country'. Here we see inspiration that is not grounded in the reality of all people in the organisation. Another example is where a change effort starts with 'we are going to create something really exciting' but after a week or two the rhetoric turns to 'we need to save money'. And yet another example is the developmental review that ideally should align personal and organisational goals but where employees come out saying, as one colleague did, 'that was the most de-motivating experience of my career'. Here we see that the systems which create the organisational reality destroy inspiration. When executive MBA students were asked what they really thought was going on in these types of situations, which were very familiar to them as managers, one student captured the overall sentiment when he said:

> We wildly swing from inspiration to reality. We know we need to be encouraging and inspiring, we want to do this, but in response to the day-to-day reality—for example, a directive from management that staff are to focus only on profit-related goals, or that there is no money for professional development—the management badge goes on and humanity is put to the side, thus even the inspirational stuff becomes 'another thing to do' not because I don't want to be human but it is as if the manager role takes over.

In this quote we note that the 'manager role', as he experienced it, had no place to hold on to inspiration when reality got too demanding. Inspiration is constantly abandoned under the pressure of survival and within organisational cultures that do not see its value, or where inspiration is seen as a luxury, only for the good times, or for certain times of the year. But where inspiration is abandoned, hope is abandoned too, and without that the workplace loses all that inspired human beings can generate.

In this first section, we look at how inspiration and reality can both be held in view in all situations, and the effect of doing this on people, teams and organisations. We start by discussing the sources of inspiration in organisations, their natural emergence and active management.

Personal inspiration in the workplace

As seen in Chapter 5, inspiration meets our human need to be uplifted, for new energy, hope and vision, for possibilities beyond the here and now. From an organisational perspective, actively managing inspiration has long been seen as a way to mobilise employees towards greater creativity and effort. In this section we first assess the nature and effectiveness of various sources of inspiration in the workplace, and then discuss what we have learned about working with inspiration in organisations in ways that support meaningfulness.

Exercise 6.1

Purpose

To explore inspiration in the context of your workplace.

Instructions

- Thinking over your current work, what is done that inspires you? (e.g. something said by others or shown through example, or ways of addressing a client or customer need).

- Now look at what is actively designed and managed by others with the intention of inspiring you (e.g. goal setting, sales targets, inspirational speech, corporate vales).

- What effect does each of these forms of inspiration have on you?

- What would make the most difference in keeping your inspiration alive?

In doing Exercise 6.1, some of you will notice that quite small things inspire you at work: things that you might create; a client, student or patient thanking you for something that makes a difference to them. It might be noticing the effect your work has on another; or a touching conversation with a colleague, or seeing a suggestion that you have made picked up by management. And it is often from such small things that new practices are developed.

For example, in children's oncology wards in Dutch hospitals it is now common practice for nurses and parents to keep a diary together. It is a way of explaining procedure and keeping each other informed about what happened during the days and nights, but it has also become a way of making present what is sometimes unspeakable. It has a tremendous effect on the relationship between caregivers and parents, and ultimately also on the quality of care. But it started with a small spark, a response to a need for a better connection between nurses and parents. One nurse started to write 'diary' notes to a parent and the parent would leave notes in return. From this arose a systematic practice, but it started with just one person feeling inspired to create a better connection, acting on her inspiration and then telling others about it.

For many, Exercise 6.1 led to conversations about making the things that inspire them more visible in their daily work:

> We are a company that creates medical equipment that makes a real difference to children who have cancer. We are of course inspired by the possibilities of improving the lives of these kids. Yet we all get caught up in the technical aspects of this work, meeting the deadlines, designing ever increasingly complex applications. Sometimes we get a letter from a parent or a kid who writes to us about the difference our equipment has made to their lives. When we talked about inspiration we decided to blow some of these letters up to poster size and put them around our workplace. We know why we are here, but we forget, and it is good to remind ourselves.

For others, this exercise led to conversations about how inspiration continues to be valuable even though often the organisation fails to fully realise the vision:

> Our purpose statement has in it that we 'contribute to a healthier society'. At times this has been challenging. Not all our current products are healthy. Also it is sometimes hard to find replacements that people want to buy or want to pay extra for. But it guides us in our new product development and gradually we are removing sugar etc. from a wider range of our products. I like the fact that we are reaching for the stars in spite of the practical difficulties we face.

There are many initiatives at an individual, group and organisational level that help to keep inspiration present and alive. Simply reconnecting with our inspiration, as a deliberate and regular practice, can help us to see how to remain attuned to what is important. As all other elements of meaning, Inspiration needs to be revitalised and reassessed on an ongoing basis. Goals are achieved or found to be misguided and new ones are created; circumstances change and may lead to inspiring opportunities.

From both examples above it is clear that everyone can be responsible for keeping inspiration alive and relevant, for themselves and in the workplace in general. Because inspiration is recognised as one of the most potent forces in mobilising people, it figures strongly in current organisational theory and practice. Most inspirational practices are focused on leadership, culture, vision and values management. However, often the real issue is power and participation. The nurse above could implement a small change initiative because she had the power to do so. Such power can be discretionary (having enough time and resources to implement new ideas) or structural (being able to try things out without having to run everything past one's manager) or participatory (being able to participate in decision-making so that what inspires a team or department can be kept alive).

At a personal level, we disempower ourselves if we wait for others to empower us, and at an organisational level, putting Inspiration in the hands of a small group of people is not only risky but also creates 'us versus them' feelings and means that many vision and mission statements are one-off events rather than living documents. In addition, Inspiration is not freely experienced when it is directed from the top. It often comes with detailed plans and KPIs, some of which destroy the very inspiration they are trying to uphold. These are all reasons for the whole of the organisation, rather than a senior management team, to be in control of inspiration.

The search for inspiration is already inherent in human beings. We are always delighted to find how naturally inspiration emerges when individuals can speak to what really matters to them and plan how they can sustain their motivation. Participants comment that this way of working with inspiration does not feel forced or, even more important, coerced or manipulative. They say it feels light, doable and energising, even in situations which have before seemed intractable.

In the following case study, we can see how the Map helped a team to feel energised where they previously had felt disempowered and how the organisation as a whole responded to the efforts of this team.

Case Study 6.1 **The team takes over**

I had been brought in to work with a team that was described as struggling in a number of ways. After working with them to find out what they considered to be the issues, and working through some ways they could be more empowered in the situation in which they found themselves, I introduced the team to the Map of Meaning. As we went through it, they could instantly see examples of the elements in their current work situation.

When I had finished, one of them said, 'We can use this Map as a way to complete all our personal plans and have them in by the end of July'. These plans had been consistently late, and the team was often the last group in the company to get their personal plans completed. They were dispirited and lacking confidence in their ability to plan. Many were also struggling with the technology involved. Their inspiration was to be the first in the organisation to get their plans in next time. As they started to work on this, the manager sat back and looked on as the team took over. As it was their suggestion to use the Map for the plans, they were fully engaged.

I asked them what was important in each element of the Map of Meaning as we went around it. Their replies are captured below. The sentence in italics is what they hoped to get from fulfilling the vision in each element.

We began with inspiration as this was the driver for the project.

Inspiration

- The achievement
- Shared success
- 'Wow, we've done it'
- Move on and maintain it.

This would give us hope that we are able to achieve things

Unity with others

- We will have to be patient with one another and share knowledge and skills
- And we will need to support each other
- And say when we are struggling and ask for help
- We need to work out together how many plans there are to do and co-operate about getting all these done
- We need to share the prize.

And doing this will create a positive team

Expressing full potential

- Each person needs to use their own strengths
- Each person has to take responsibility for being prepared
- Each person needs to develop their skills so that we are all competent

- We need to become unconsciously competent at these skills so there is less resistance to working with technology.

This would give us a marvellous sense of accomplishment

Integrity with self

- We need to be willing to take the challenge on
- Be committed
- Remind ourselves in a practical way that there is support available
- Be honest enough to ask for help.

This would increase our sense of meaning and also confidence

Serving others

- Frees up our energy to work more effectively with clients
- We can be more focused on client goals
- We can be better partners to the client
- We can give quality support.

This would develop our competence, wisdom and ability to serve our clients

Reality

- We need to set time aside to do the learning, teaching and actual plans
- We need to be clear on how it would be achieved
- We need measures to keep on track
- We need to set it as part of the staff agenda each week so that we can keep connected with the goal.

And, the outcome was that they achieved this. The team was jubilant at what they had accomplished and shared the prize of a chocolate cake from Head Office.

Clearly, in this case the team did not think it was unreasonable for Head Office to ask for plans, but the request had become a burden to the team. In such cases, there would have been many other ways to get the same result, such as setting deadlines and consequences, blaming each other, or the manager taking over the planning process. But in this case, using the Map helped to breathe life into the planning process, and helped the team to draw on what they already knew would help them to commit as a team. This knowledge, we find, is almost always present. The Map helps to draw it out, in language that is owned by those having to make it happen, which makes it easy for them to do. In using the Map, it was natural for the team to take over and the manager to sit back.

Reality of Self and Circumstances in the workplace

As we saw in many of the earlier quotes and examples, reality, both of ourselves and of our circumstances, comes naturally to the fore when we talk about what inspires us. While people may experience the reality of themselves differently inside and outside the workplace, the key to meaningful work is how we confront, accept and work with the reality of our selves and circumstances. From the case study above, we can see that these are not separate. Often, where there are blockages to getting things done in organisations, they are a combination of individual, team and systems factors. As above, the team members themselves had started to avoid the issue, become dispirited and lost confidence. In such circumstances there are a few team members who are able to inspire themselves and others by saying something like, 'Come on guys, we can do this'. At the same time, the computer system itself was not helping, and often there are such obstacles to what can be useful, and meaningful, tasks. In the next section we further investigate where the organisational reality gets in the way of meaningful work.

Exercise 6.2

Purpose

To explore the impact of circumstances on your inspiration.

Instructions

- At work where do you (collectively) spend most of your time working towards the purpose of the organisation and where do you spend your time battling what is at hand? Where are you putting out fires and where have you made progress towards a common goal? Are you spending most of your time on the things that inspire you or do other things get in the way?

- Is there one specific circumstance that has arisen that challenges you, or does it 'all just seem too hard'?
- What ways do people at work have to support themselves in keeping going?
- What do you suspect may continue to defeat them?

What participants in our workshop have noticed depends on the organisation in which they work. There is a (usually small) group that feels aligned with the overall purpose of the organisation and experiences a collective energy as a result. For example, 'we are small and smart and save our customers 15 per cent of their electricity bill every winter'. Of course, this really does make a difference, particularly to older and poorer customers.

Often there is a group that feels aligned with the purpose of the organisation but feels that the daily battle for resources, the daily demands of the job or the daily battle to simply be listened to, or have one's expertise acknowledged, saps their energy. For example, 'I used to feel I really helped people finding the best electricity deal, and I still do, but with the new regulations there is so much paperwork involved and when this creates anxiety in the customer I'm sometimes thinking, "just stay put, why bother switching?"'.

Then there is a group that feels that what the organisation is striving for is unrealistic, not shared, and not consistently lived. As one of our workshop participants, who works for an electricity company, said:

> On the one hand, we had these wonderful leadership programmes in which we were encouraged to live by our principles. On the other hand, if there was a price increase, no one would ask how this would affect our poorest customers.

Finally there is a group (again, usually small) that is not at all aligned or no longer aligned with how the organisation defines its reason for existence, saying, for example, 'I am no longer interested in getting people to switch from another electricity company to ours, I just don't see how it improves people's lives', and who quite often end up saying, 'Well, I don't care about all this purpose and meaning stuff, I come to work to pay the bills'.

What we have noticed is that people do not usually struggle with the fact that a gap between inspiration and reality exists. They expect it. What drains their energy is when they feel they cannot talk about it openly and honestly. Or they cannot participate in decisions on how to make things better, or they do not believe that resources are being used for the right purposes. Often this results in people expressing their resistance in cynical ways, silently internalising their frustrations, and withdrawing their discretionary labour.

What we have learned in working with Reality of Circumstances

Reality can be the graveyard of corporate dreams and aspirations. Reality can so easily lead to cynicism, bitterness, feeling overwhelmed and despair – all expressions of frustrated inspiration. Yet reality can be the source of inspiration as well. Examples where the boss and senior managers take huge pay cuts in order to keep people in jobs, or where everyone agrees to shorter hours and less pay in order to maintain their colleagues in employment, or where managers are humble and really start drawing on the collective rather than paying lip service to empowerment, can create an inspiring organisational culture that is at the same time real.

Time and again we found that having Reality present in the Map of Meaning legitimises people talking about it without judgement or negativity, and supports them participating in solutions which has a profound and lasting effect, as we see in Case study 6.2 where a certified practitioner describes one way he uses the Map.

Case Study 6.2 **Reality beyond negativity**

I have worked with the Map of Meaning as a facilitator for a number of years. In this organisation I was particularly drawn to its ability as a reflective tool to deepen self-awareness while delivering a long programme of personal leadership development as part of organisational training within the police. I used the map focusing on the three axes of Being/Doing, Self/Others and Inspiration/Reality.

However, for many of them the key issue was centred on the axis of Inspiration and Reality. They struggled to accept and work with reality. They got bogged down in things not being as they should, fighting what is, rather than learning that it is not helpful, resisting the deep spiritual truth of living in the present and accepting and working with what is. That's understandable because there's a great fear that if they accept things as they are, they'll lose what they stand for. When they saw Inspiration and Reality out there in the PowerPoint diagram, and they graphically perceived the relation between the two—which is virtually impossible to explain verbally—they experienced both the release of seeing their circumstances outside of themselves (these are real and shared) but at the same time, they realised: 'So this is what is'. And then they began to ask themselves, 'So what am I going to do and how am I going to work with it?' They experienced this as a real empowerment.

In my many years of working with people across a very broad variety of roles and organisations I have found that people often get stuck in 'drama triangles' (cf. transactional analysis). In organisations it's easy to get stuck in the drama triangle, whether in the position of 'victim' (or, in rapid switches of position, to 'persecutor' and/or 'rescuer' at times too). By focusing on the bigger areas offered by the Map of Meaning, within the context of Reality and Inspiration, it helped them to get unstuck. They connected with a deeper part of themselves. People want to be grounded. They don't want to remain stuck in the drama triangle. The Map of Meaning takes them to somewhere where they aren't stuck, to a place where they can access that non-neurotic part of themselves. It takes them deeper and they connect with areas of deep purpose, rather than the more superficial stuff.

This is often subtle but profound, and often meets with very positive feedback from participants:

> The Map of Meaning was interesting to use not peruse, if you get what I mean? It wasn't until I started to articulate the words that I found my way around the Map in a useful/directional way. It took me from reality to inspiration and back again many times. I found I spent a lot of time in contributing (Doing/Others quadrant). The questions, which were mainly organisational (e.g. What am I doing to bring back inspiration?), have set me thinking. On reflection I now wonder why I haven't spent more time in Development and Self-actualisation quadrants over the past 18 months, though I am aware Self is low in my priorities when there is work to be done. All in all, a very useful reflective tool. It also increased the level of trust and honesty within the team.

Again, here we see that the Map naturally bridges the personal and the organisational. It creates trust and a feeling of coming to terms with what one has control over. As the practitioner reflects, 'The "ought to's", are so strong in public sector cultures because of their close connection to values. But they can stop people being connected and authentic because they speak to a politically correct facade, rather than their work as they experience it. When people acknowledge what that is, no matter how fearful, they access their true potential to move on. When both inspiration and reality are confronted by everyone, the team can more easily pull together, rather than being locked into one or other position through their personal preference or by the cultural norms.'

This is empowering and necessary in organisations, because if reality is not faced head on, conflict often arises. The following case study example shows how the Map helps to face reality head on.

Case Study 6.3 **Facing reality head on**

A practitioner was drawn to use the Map of Meaning in conflict because, 'What I see is that conflict is triggered when something that's really important to people is threatened, or hindered. So, I saw the connection with the Map because it captures what truly matters to people. And it allows for diversity because what is hindered or threatened can be different for different people. The Map gives us a way to look at all of this.

My brief was to facilitate a restorative conversation with a future focus, to rebuild what had been a cohesive team, identify any barriers to this, and identify the next steps that we all have to take.

I started with the lead question, (which people were asked to consider before they arrived), which was: "What has gone missing that truly matters to you?"

They had to write these down on separate sticky notes, select the one that was most important to them and put that in a basket (this way no-one could see who contributed what). I asked people to move into small groups and I handed out the stickies. They had to look at the key words and assign them to a place on the map.

For example, under:

- **Unity with Others**: they put, Trust, Support for each Other; with Communication and Openness as a link between Unity and Service to Others
- **Service to Others**: Management Support
- **Expressing Full Potential**: People being Committed to their Jobs, Responsibility
- **Integrity with Self:** Stability, Faith and Confidence; with Respect and Empathy linking this with Unity with Others.

It was not important that they got it "right" but that they had a discussion. The Map was so valuable because it helped structure and frame the situation and make it legitimate to say what was missing. It also created a sense of order, which is so important especially in conflict when everything seems so totally muddled.

I'd summarise the benefit as people able to say:

- I am not standing in nothing and saying this, I am standing in the Map and saying this
- The Map understands me, the Map gives me legitimacy
- The Map has created an orderly way of thinking
- The Map shows me where I stand and where other people stand
- Other people are in other places, but they are also standing in the Map.

This conversation and process alone created a level of understanding about others' experiences. Restorative justice assumes that impact is a motivator for change, so I asked them to go into small groups and discuss:

- What happens if that is missing?
- What happens to you, others and the organisation when this is missing?

And this was clear because if, for example, communication is missing, then Unity with Others is missing. This is powerful because people see the cost to them, and also see that their upset is contained in just the few dimensions of the Map, so it becomes manageable which gives people the energy to look for solutions.

Next I did a mini presentation on what happens in times of change and conflict, separate from the Map. This led to the idea of being and doing your best for yourself and others in the midst of change and challenge. In the light of this we discussed the sticky notes on the Map.

For each key word people had to think of what strategies we could do to restore what was missing and truly matters to them. This was very engaging, because it was their words on the Map. They could see their own words but also what they had in common. So important, because in conflict people are often locked in binary viewpoints. The Map legitimises their position, which frees them up to see how it legitimises other points of view at the same time. They can see that meaning consists of multiple dimensions, which can be enacted in multiple ways, and in fact all contribute something.

We then looked at the strategies and decided on the things that we really needed to agree on.

Many people were very reluctant to come to the session, but at the end they all felt it had been worthwhile. They had begun to see that conflict is normal'.

Working with the Map allows people to talk about reality and inspiration as they experience it. This enables them to constructively discuss the experienced world through questions such as: What's it really like to use this day to day? Does it help or hinder in us making a difference? Do staff have ways to extend themselves in using the system or do they experience themselves as passive respondents? Does the system support or replace the experience of quality human interaction? Does the system in reality create an experience of loss of integrity through, e.g., people taking shortcuts on important issues?

Next we explore the experience of too much reality.

Too much reality

Recently one of us was in a meeting of an organisation that had decided to become more sustainable. A project group had been appointed to be in charge of the sustainability agenda. They had organised a meeting to obtain staff input.

Many people offered ideas but within a time-span of 20 minutes we heard: 'Let's be real here', said by three different people; 'Nice idea, but in the real world', from seven different people; and 'We can't even consider such an idea with the budget constraints we're facing', also mentioned by three people.

If the audience had been a balloon one could have seen it deflate and after about 20 minutes people simply stopped offering ideas. These phrases, which we have all heard many times, are ways of using reality as a bludgeon. It does not only kill innovation and creativity – the very things organisations say they are desperate for – but it also goes straight to the heart of our humanity. It says, 'you can only be human if you grow up and see the world for what it is – my way,' and, 'you are not allowed to dream about future possibilities for the world'.

On another occasion, we observed a meeting in which a seaport company had invited the community to a meeting. The community wanted input into what was to be done with soon-to-be-vacated areas of harbour access. The community was told that, in principle, the port was not against consultation but only if they could 'make mature contributions that would be real'. Here, too, reality was framed as the domain of 'grown-ups', the domain of the serious and the successful who then get to define reality for everyone else.

In these cases the way reality is used is almost as a punishment for daring to dream or have an idea of anything other than business as usual. Used in this way, it becomes an excuse, a way of not engaging with or taking any action on the more challenging aspects of organisational life, or of ignoring possible new ways of doing things. It's so endemic that many people have stopped offering their ideas. Thus we have the ironic situation where organisations spend money on programmes designed to encourage creativity and innovation and then wonder why nothing happens. A few words can stop most creativity and innovation before they are born. One group is left feeling permanently frustrated while another has a sense of being the only one who sees things 'as they really are'. In all these cases 'reality' simply prevents us from listening harder and helping to contribute a glimmer of an idea that might bear valuable fruit if given a bit more time and attention.

Finally, reality can become too hard to engage with. There are situations where employees see that managers have taken decisions that suck the inspiration from their jobs, even when employees have put in a lot of their own time and emotional labour working through badly thought-out ideas. At some point, employees abandon the search for meaning simply to stay sane and survive. In such situations, meaning can no longer be found at work, and the wisest thing to do is to protect one's health and well-being by emotionally (and also in terms of extra hours put in) withdrawing from the organisation to use time and energy to find meaning in other life roles. This happens so regularly in our experience, with the cost of this to the organisation being virtually incalculable.

Too little reality

While too much reality can suck the meaning out of work, so does too much talk of inspiration without being connected to reality. We have all been in a meeting listening to some person rave on about an idea that feels off the planet and found ourselves wanting them to 'get real'. Some motivational speakers sound almost hysterical because they seem completely detached from the world as we know it. But more often in organisations employees are asked to go along with a type of pretence about the organisation living by its vision statement, that people are treated as its most important asset, or that the organisation is concerned about more than profit. Yet employees feel that they cannot articulate constructively how changes will affect them, that there are not true processes in place to consult on very real concerns they have about how changes will affect their workload or their job security, or to measure the impact these changes will have on them over time. In such situations meaning is lost because a mockery has been made of what most employees do in fact hold dear.Douglas Ready and Jay Conger (2008), who have researched why bold visions and inspirational leadership acts fail in organisations, describe the story of a meeting of a large international finance company. The scene was carefully set; 3,500 executives had been flown in for the purpose, loud music and laser images peppered the crowd and the stage:

> The message was simple: 'We will become "the breakout firm". And to achieve breakout status we will rely on the three I's of innovation, integration, and inspiration'. Given the tight schedule of events for this one-day meeting, the CEO took no questions. But the speech had caught the executives' attention, and the new vision created a buzz of excitement.
>
> Months later, the buzz had worn off. Reality had intruded, as it always does ... In short, following their initial enthusiasm the company's senior executives were having a hard time reconciling the new vision with day-to-day realities.
>
> Ready and Conger 2008

This will feel very familiar to many employees and managers: vision is easy, the slog is getting there, with the real issue being the process of getting there: who is in the know, who gets sidelined, who can be trusted. Just as reality is always present in our personal lives, so it is in the workplace. When we focus on inspiration to the exclusion of the reality, or reality at the exclusion of inspiration, we run the risk of not accessing creativity (too much reality) or are unable to ground inspiration and make it work (too little reality). The first leads to resignation and the second to cynicism, both of which currently infest far too many organisations. While the gap is a normal part of organising, when it cannot be articulated it frustrates the human need to contribute to and participate in meaningful work.

The trick is to work with both in view, and that is where a process of participation, using the Map of Meaning, helps constructively connect the daily experience of workers with both inspiration and reality, and the systems in which they work.

Working with Inspiration and Reality in organisations

Inspiration and Reality can so easily appear as opposing forces. However, at an organisational level, working constructively with reality can also provide inspiration. In the following case study, we can see how a circumstance that was negatively impacting an organisation became a great strength based on the use of the Map as a strategic planning process.

Case Study 6.4 **Making a virtue of reality**

One practitioner was asked to work with a small public service organisation supplying service to sick and disabled people in rural areas. The reality of this organisation, which they were struggling with, was a four monthly funding cycle which had virtually destroyed inspiration because they had no sense of a secure future to which they could aspire.

Working for a day with the Map as a strategic planning tool turned this situation around. First, they surfaced their genuine shared passion for their work. This gave them a strong base for looking at the reality of the challenge. They realised that the funding cycle left them feeling powerless, so they started to focus on what they could influence and control and decided to create a three-year vision and then work to ensure that the funding would be there. They saw this as being pro-active in creating the future they were committed to, so that they could reconnect with and express their passion for their work and the contribution it made. This immediately released their motivation.

Working with the four pathways as a method to develop creative solutions they realised it would make sense to create a really positive, long-term relationship with their funder (who was currently seen as 'the enemy'). They worked through the services they offered and saw that these were huge and varied and decided to focus on a more limited but essential suite of services instead. They left the day, connected, inspired and with practical actions to take.

When I met them a few months later they had indeed transformed their relationship with the funder who now saw them as an exemplar organisation, because they were clear in their vison, practical in the range of services they offer, and inspired in their work. The day had strengthened all the internal relationships among people who often work remotely, and re-energised each individual to be part of creating new and better ways of offering the essential services. They now refer to their strategic plan as 'Our Map of Meaning'. Of course funding will always be at the whim of the provider, but the team felt that even if they did not get future funding, they would be more at peace with that as they were now very clear of the contributions they had made, regardless of future decisions that were out of their control.

Working with the Map helps open up opportunities for everyone to take charge of meaning. As we can see in the examples above, it does not have to be left to the CEO. Working with the Map helps reduce the responsibility on CEOs and senior managers and helps them find their boundaries, as those working with senior managers reflect.

> I find that they are actually often trying to do too much. The Map helps them find their boundaries, clarify what is their responsibility and let go what isn't. When they let go, others can step up and develop themselves.

This also challenges the sense that inspiration must flow from the leader and supports more collective concepts of everyone as leader. It demonstrates that with the will of the whole group a very disempowering situation can be transformed.

While we have referred to this throughout the chapter, we want to draw attention to the power of the Map of Meaning to help people constructively speak about the gap between inspiration and reality. At the start of this chapter we showed a simple model showing that much managerial energy goes into putting the systems in place to achieve the purpose. In this next case study we can see that doing this resulted in some real problems, leaving staff feeling vulnerable and defensive. Using the Map of Meaning enabled the facilitator to raise the issues so that nobody lost face and solutions were easily found.

Case Study 6.5 Working constructively and gently in challenging situations

One certified practitioner was working in a developing country with a professional group which was consistently failing to achieve a specific aspect of their work. She wanted to work with the group in a way that felt safe and respectful of their professionalism. With their boss present, she introduced the Map and then asked the group to talk about what had inspired them to join the office.

Everyone explained their reasons for joining and talked about what drew them to the role. The whole room just filled up, you could almost see it. The boss was moved and said how touched she was to hear all these stories, how it reminded her what wonderful staff they had. She then told the story of what had inspired her to work in this office, which in turn moved her staff.

We had a break and then I asked them to talk about Reality, by asking, 'so this is what inspired you, what is the reality like?'

This created the opportunity for them to talk about how fearful they were in the early weeks of work and how they felt deserted when their supervisor left them to do their job on their own after only one week of training.

This discussion, of both the inspiration and the reality of their experience, formed the basis for them to work with the Map to devise some creative and practical solutions to the initial problem.

As we have suggested previously, the Map can be used in many different ways. Particularly with challenging situations, it can be very helpful to use it on the floor and ask people to physically move through it. This helps draw out intuitive knowledge, but not having to speak also sometimes makes it easier to make tensions visible to others without confronting anyone.

After lunch, with the Map on the floor, I asked them to explore their work by walking around the Map. All of them stood in Inspiration and then took a giant step, right over the four pathways to Reality. When they walked through the four pathways they all had their own order, their own sequence of doing this.

They looked at their main problem through all the pathways of the Map, focusing particularly on what the experience was like for their clients. By the end of the workshop, the participants talked about how the issue was not just their own lack of training but that the real issue was that they had to make their clients fill out very difficult forms and neither the employees nor the clients knew how to do this, yet the form had significant consequences for the client. As a result, they knew they were not making enough of a difference in spite of the best intentions.

People realised that the existing rules, the bureaucratic threshold, made it impossible for both employees and clients to put their best effort forward. But because no-one was labelled 'wrong' and concrete connections between the meaning of service and the organisational practices were made, they could easily identify the next step. They went back to the original legislation to clarify the original intention, and both the training and forms were changed.

The practitioner commented, 'I found that the Map was so gentle, there was no blame. Everybody told their own story and everybody listened. It helped people to talk about their emotions *and* their work in ways that were comfortable, useful, and in a space where they felt safe, which increased empathy and which supported their professionalism'.

We can see in this case study that the forms were designed with the intention of achieving the organisational purpose. The underlying assumption being, 'if we put the systems in place, our purpose will be met'. However, in the world experienced by the employees (the world where motivation and demotivation is deeply felt), the forms were actually inhibiting the organisational purpose. In identifying this and the resultant lack of meaning, it was immediately obvious to everyone what needed to be done next.

We can see that a combination of connecting administrative tasks to real-world meaning and outcomes, expressing feelings in terms of lack of meaning and a desire for meaning, and having the boss present, led to an important systems change. The Map helps to connect the purpose and the system, through the experience of those working with the system, instantly reconnecting them with the meaningfulness of their work.

The final exercise of this chapter is deliberately set out to bring about systems change.

Taking collective responsibility between Inspiration and Reality

In Chapter 5 we saw that taking responsibility is absolutely essential to living meaningfully. However, organisations present an interesting challenge to this. On the one hand, organisations want responsible individuals who are proactive, accountable and mature. On the other hand, organisational processes that discourage employee participation in decision making often suggest that, while employee responsibility is desired, there is doubt over whether employees can be trusted to act responsibly. This has led to extensive management, controls, and decisions being made that lead to bogus empowerment. Employees cannot influence the system but are 'empowered' to decide how to approach tasks or jobs, including the implementation of things with which they fundamentally disagree. Employees often respond with anger, blame and co-dependency to which the organisational response is to put more management and control in place, resulting in a vicious cycle. It is in this complex context that we examine how the Map can help all members of the organisation to take collective responsibility.

Exercise 6.3

Purpose

To participate in setting meaningful objectives and to evaluate these in meaningful ways.

Instructions

- Go back to one of the most recent values or change exercises your organisation did. This could be writing a strategic plan, setting a mission, outlining the reasons for change, revisiting a vision or values statements or initiating training programmes on teamwork or integrity.
- Evaluate the extent to which everyone:
  - Participated in arriving at these values, ideals or purposes.
  - Is clear on the reasons why certain courses of action need to occur.
  - Is currently participating in upholding them.

The chances are your organisation has a written set of values. Around 80 per cent of all companies and not-for-profit organisations have such statements. These values can describe attitudes or ways of doing things, as well as ideal outcomes such as 'teamwork', 'the customer is always right', 'employees are valued above all else' or 'integrity'. In many cases the values are prescribed by management, and employees are given training to develop their understanding of these values. In other cases a more bottom-up approach is taken, in which employees are asked what they consider to be the most important values that the organisation already has or should strive for. These are then collated and, usually with the aid of communication experts, written down in a way that combines all input but that, unfortunately, is often no longer recognised by employees as their own. A human resources manager in a company that tries to be values-driven, reported after doing this exercise:

> The CEO asked me to collate what employees valued in this company and also what they felt should be the overall values and purpose statement of this company. We went through some extensive consultation with various groups of employees, ensuring they all had some input. A few days later the CEO emailed 'can you just get some of those phrases to me and I'll pick the most relevant, positive and telling examples and arrive at a statement'.

We came across only a very small number of research participants who had examples where the whole process was co-owned. We also came across many cases where the values were upheld when convenient to certain parties and ignored when not convenient.

In the following case the certified practitioner worked with both the board and staff of a small organisation.

Case Study 6.6 **Using the Map of Meaning with values**

A client, a small organisation very focused on survival, as many small organisations are, decided that it needed to be clear on its culture and values as part of marketing itself better and improving organisational cohesion.

I used the Map of Meaning to work with values identified by a range of stakeholders.

In the session I briefly explained the Map by asking them what makes their work meaningful to them. They filled the sections on Expressing Full Potential and Services to Others – they are a training establishment. There were fewer comments in Unity with Others and Integrity with Self. They were interested in this, but not concerned as the organisation has a tight and supportive culture, there is room for individual development and their focus is on doing.

We then put, one by one, the three cultural values that they rated as most important in the centre of the Map, as a source of inspiration. We worked through each element of the Map in the light of this inspirational value. Doing this highlighted just how deeply embedded the value was in the culture, what really supported the expression of the value, and what was missing or making it difficult to achieve. For example, they were completely committed to being a first-class training institution. In going through the four pathways with this value in mind, they saw that while the staff felt a great deal of unity, at times there had been a rift between students and instructors, largely created by the way 'honest feedback' had been perceived by the students. This led to a discussion about how to create more trust between the two groups, while still teaching to the highest level which does require honest feedback. This led to them planning to learn to give and receive feedback more effectively, both systemically and individually.

Another outcome was to look more clearly at their student interview and selection process. They realised that they were committed to producing the highest calibre of students and that they could tell in the initial interview whether students are committed to this, or whether they want to be spoon-fed. But their current process did not focus on this, so they revised their interview and selection process.

The session enabled the CEO and Board members to hear from the staff about what is and is not working in relation to the key cultural values, and they all got to work on solutions. Most importantly, as a whole group they identified and now own these values, and are clear what they mean in daily practice. These are not values that just stay posted on the wall, but values that are embedded and demonstrated in daily life.

Value-identification practices hold great promise and considerable resources are often invested in them. Both employees and managers have opportunities to articulate what is important to them as human beings, and many argue (Sinek 2009) that these statements can increase accountability, clarify expectations and increase employee pride and commitment.

At the same time, it is important to use processes such as the Map to ensure collective input and collective responsibility for deciding why the organisation exists and whether it is living up to this purpose. This is becoming particularly important because organisations go through many change processes. Change requires significant amounts of time and energy. When the organisation cannot explain the 'why' of the change, or constantly shifts the why's, it is not possible for employees to experience meaningful work.

In the above example the Map connects the Purpose and the Systems, by identifying meaningful processes. It is these processes that employees experience on a day to day basis and that are needed to fulfil all dimensions of meaning. It has long been understood that when values are not co-created there is no buy-in, but what is less well understood is that employees don't need to just buy into the values, but also into the processes that enact such values, as these processes are their day to day experience of meaning. Co-creation can be an unwieldy process, hard to facilitate well and the fear of this means that many organisations set up steering committees, which often, intentionally or unintentionally, block collective consultation and participation. The Map makes it easier to solicit or offer a focused contribution and makes all parties feel safe. It leads to practical outcomes, solutions that employees immediately connect to, and can test through, their own experience. Clearly, when the intention is to keep employees in the dark, or simply have them follow orders, it is not appropriate to use the Map!

In the previous example we looked at how the Map helps in acting on, or refining, parts of missions statements. In this final section we look at a case study in which the Map of Meaning is used to collectively arrive at and implement a mission statement for the whole of the organisation. We introduce it in the light of current literature which asks why so many values exercises fall short of their intentions.

Inspiration and reality from the bottom up

As the interest of the scholarly and business communities in 'the management of meaning' has developed, questions have been raised about whether healthy outcomes for individuals and society are achieved when meaning becomes a form of normative control—that is, a way to keep people in line (Willmott 1993; Casey 1999; Ashforth and Vaidyanath 2002). Organisations have increasingly found that such forms of control are counterproductive; they just do not achieve the desired levels of buy-in. 'The management of meaning' may in fact reduce the experience of meaningful work. Meaninglessness arises when meaning is either substituted or controlled, because, in both cases, it is no longer authentic for the individual or the group. Sievers (1994: 26–7) writes:

> As meaning gets lost (and with it the ability or quality of meaning as a coordinating and integrating source for one's own actions as well as for the interactions with others) motivation has to be invented. Through motivation the lack of meaning of work becomes substituted or converted into the question 'how does one get people to act and produce under conditions in which they normally would not be 'motivated' to work?'.

The question that scholars and practitioners then asked was, 'how do we empower people?'. A lot of discussion about empowerment followed. However, this has led to what is referred to as bogus empowerment (Ciulla 2000). For example, Parry and Bryman (2006: 447), in summarising leadership research from the mid-1980s until the time of their research, noticed that leadership is still 'seen as a process whereby the leader identifies for subordinates a sense of what is important – defining organisational reality for others' and where 'the leader gives a sense of direction and of purpose through the articulation of a compelling world-view'. If this vision is not provided by the leader, it is usually done so by a consultant. The ongoing preoccupation with culture change has 'meant the elaboration of new programmes embodied in mission statements, visions and new value systems facilitated by a plethora of consultancy interventions, aimed at reinventing both the identity of the corporation and of the subjects within it' (Costea *et al.* 2008: 661).

However, cracks have begun to appear in this top-down or externally guided approach to the management of meaning. Many organisations are looking for alternatives. They realise they have to find better ways to connect personal and organisational meaning.

It is increasingly recognised that everyone needs to share a purpose for the organisation to be able to deliver on it. Otherwise it will fail and destroy meaningful work for most members of the organisation. In the next case study we show how the Map enables a bottom-up vision statement in which all employees are involved.

The following case study spans four years of a certified practitioner's experiences with one organisation.

Case Study 6.7 **A bottom-up vision statement**

I always use the Map in several stages. First I focus on connecting the individual to what is meaningful to them personally. Next I focus on the individual's role in the organisation. Then I focus on the organisation itself. I have found it makes a big difference if you ask the individual to reflect on what is meaningful for them before you start to focus on the organisation because the organisation can only be whole to the extent that the individuals within it are whole.

When you get individuals to focus on the needs of the organisation without getting them to focus on themselves, they still have the question of 'what about me' going on, and rightly so. So you might as well get that on the table first. When people have been able to attend to what is meaningful to them personally, they bring peace to the process.

If the individual feels nourished throughout the process they find a richness and quality in their contributions. They operate from a higher place.

In subsequent sessions I have seen that this really helps people to connect the personal to the organisational and back again. It makes it so easy to generate the practical expression of such things as a vision and mission statement because people are already so connected to it.

In the next stage, we focused on the organisational vision. In this case the members of the board and paid staff were involved. For the process, we used brainstorming. People came up with words that were important to them, made sentences, used dictionaries, etc. It was a vibrant process and we kept paring back from a huge amount of words. People kept focusing on how they were going as a group while also checking in with how they were doing themselves. All the words and sentences were eventually pared back to a single statement that said, 'a vibrant place of hope and connection, standing tall, reaching all'.

One of the things that also became apparent was that the paid workers had a vision they had not shared with the board. For this reason it was so important to have everyone, regardless of their position, involved in this process. As one of the board directors wrote: 'This day captured the needs of the organisation, helped us to focus and prioritise and re-energised and renewed the vision and purpose of our existence . . . thank you, we all took away something special for ourselves as well as some great thinking for the organisation. We have our vision statement proudly displayed and have already used it in one of our funding applications'.

I worked with the community group over the next few years and am still doing so with an annual strategic planning and review day. We use the Map less overtly as it has become integrated into what they do. It was used to decide whom they wanted to attract as new board members and to more clearly define the role of volunteers, coming up with a job description for the volunteers using the qualities from the Map.

Some outcomes:

- The vision statement was used the next day in a funding application.
- The city council adopted some of the board's vision in their own 2025 community development plan.
- The community organisation has gone from strength to strength.

As one of the staff members wrote: 'I feel we have developed wonderful, safe, practical systems that simply nourish and wow my work and workplace. Thank you, it never feels like training'.

CEOs often recognise that they need to get everyone in the organisation on board, and increasingly look at how to do so both with regard to what the organisation is (Inspiration) and is not (Reality) delivering. For example, Jeff Hollender, co-founder of Seventh Generation Inc., describes a situation (Hollender and Breen 2010) in which he felt his organisation should be transparent about the failure of one of its products to meet in-house environmental standards. The leadership team resisted this proposal on the grounds that they saw no reason to share the information and were fearful of a backlash from competitors. Hollender realised that, as deeply committed as he was to transparency as a moral principle, he had forgotten to share this vision in an effective way with his team: 'I hadn't brought anyone along with me by facilitating discussions, providing education and context about what we were about to do'. On reflection, he writes, 'What most clearly emerged from this often excruciating process was that the discussions and debates regarding what constituted a meaningful and beneficial level of disclosure were, in and of themselves, worthwhile, and were indeed drivers of change'.

Unfortunately, a year after the book was published Hollender was dismissed as CEO. In giving a speech at the sustainable brands conference he reflected on what happened: 'How did I fail? How did I get myself fired? I didn't institutionalize values in the corporate structure; I took too much money from the wrong people; I failed to give enough of the company to the employees who would have protected what we'd built; I failed to create a truly sustainable brand'. Because these elements were not in place, Hollender lost power and was unable to maintain his vision for the company. All of these issues point towards not connecting the purpose and the systems to the world of employee experience. This is where values are enacted and tested every day and where resilient and inspiring organisations are created and sustained by all members of the organisation.

It has become increasingly well documented that the members of an organisation need to take collective responsibility for purpose. For organisations to outperform others, they need to have the courage to challenge long-held management beliefs about human nature and employees, and radically depart from the traditional command-and-control structures, rules and policies. People who are not treated as equals will leave you alone with your vision. The organisation must let people self-direct and grow (Carney and Getz 2009).

Summary

- The processes that we, and many of our colleagues have developed start from an emancipatory world-view. People, especially when given the time to reflect and consult, know what is meaningful and meaningless, what they wish and do not wish to contribute their life force to. The Map of Meaning gives permission to everyone to articulate this and provides a gentle, inclusive way to work with both inspiration and reality. When people work from meaning, they work constructively towards keeping the vision alive through all that reality can throw at them.

- The two-step individual-collective process as described in Case Study 6.7 profoundly connects personal and organisational purpose, which helps peel things back to what is simple and doable. This leads to values statements that are real and have everyone's buy-in. And as we see from the case studies, people immediately take steps to put the vision into action and steps to evaluate (on a regular basis) how everyone in the organisation is living up to it.

- In this chapter we discussed how the experience of meaning and meaninglessness takes place between heaven and earth, gravity and grace, that which we strive for and where we fall short, individually and collectively. From the examples we saw it is important to normalise this, otherwise meaningfulness becomes equated with positivity, and, paradoxically, loses its profoundness. As organisations are inevitably falling short of our inspiration, hopes and ideals, it is important that all members of the organisation participate in safeguarding the ideal. This can only happen if *all* members of the organisation engage with both inspiration *and* reality.

- In an organisational context, Inspiration (the purpose of the organisation) and Reality (the systems through which the purpose is enacted) are connected through the human world of experience (on a day-to-day, week-to-week, month-to-month basis). The Map legitimises and gives powerful expression to this world of experience. This enables both those at the top and those at the bottom to connect purpose to systems by collectively negotiating and evaluating the processes that connect the purpose and the system. These systems can then be evaluated by those who created them, who are now fully responsible for the purpose and their own experience of meaningful work.

In the next chapter we will address how the Map helps to integrate the often fragmented messages and practices in organisations.

7

Speaking to meaning within organisational systems

In the previous chapter we showed the power of sharing responsibility for organisational purpose with all members of the organisation. In this chapter we show how the Map of Meaning enables this to happen, by giving everyone a simple framework to use their own words to speak about their experience of the systems in which, and with which, they work.

While there is already evidence of the importance of articulating the world of experience beyond emotions, energy, habits and power, there is a huge gap between what is known and what is done in most organisations. Until now, this is understandable, because as we have seen, the human experience of work has been pushed aside as 'messy', compared to the more easily discussed 'hard' world of results. We have not had an easy way to integrate these two worlds. The Map of Meaning enables this integration by keeping the reality of organisational needs visible while also enabling the feelings of people meeting these needs, to remain in sight.

We start by discussing the evidence of the value of employee involvement and then go on to share our experience of how the Map of Meaning can in practice assist this.

Research showing that meaningful work results in positive human and organisational outcomes

Research has already established that an organisation benefits if people experience meaningful work. The benefits include increasing commitment, job enjoyment, feelings of accomplishment or growth, positive self-concept, organisational identification, knowledge sharing, organisational citizenship and enhanced morale (Bailey *et al.* 2016).

In addition to numerous organisational and personal benefits from meaningful work, there are a number of organisational conditions that support meaningful work. Kahn and Fellows (2013) summarise a number of practices that have been derived from theory, supported by research and tested in practice. We placed the dimensions of meaningful work in brackets after each condition to show that each dimension is likely to require distinct organisational prerequisites. Kahn and Fellows (2013 p. 120) suggests that to cultivate meaningful work the organisation needs to:

- involve employees appropriately in diagnosing and solving problems (expressing full potential);

- create, authorize and support small groups and teams to take on important assignments (expressing full potential, as well as unity with others);

- develop reviews that allow for ongoing discussions about the employees' sense of purpose and meaning in relation to their work and roles (integrity with self; expressing full potential);

- build organizational communities that provide members with a sense of belonging, connectedness and meaningful attachments (unity with others);

- create structures and processes to link employees' roles and tasks to larger missions and purposes (serving others).

At the level of roles and tasks, Pratt *et al.* (2013) suggest that meaning can be cultivated through job design that:

- focuses on mastery, competence, quality and autonomy (expressing full potential);

- or that considers the relational design of the job through task interdependence and team-based designs (unity with others).

Others have researched conditions that make work meaningless. Bailey and Madden (2016) found that disconnecting people from their values (diminishing development of inner self), giving people pointless work to do and overriding people's better judgement (diminishing expression of full potential) or disconnecting people from supportive relationships (diminishing unity) leads to meaningless work.

Together with others, we believe that from a research perspective, we know most of what needs to be known about creating meaningful work and avoiding meaningless work. What we know far less about is how to move organisations from what is technically and theoretically known, to what is done in practice. To bridge this gap it is vital for everybody in the organisation to have words to speak about what matters most to them, so that it can be collectively protected.

As we have seen throughout this book, having words to speak about what matters most helps people to not only recognise their need for meaning, but to talk about it. It helps in getting a handle on the world of experience in organisations:

> I take it as an elemental truth of life that words matter. This is so plain that we can ignore it a thousand times a day. The words we use shape how we understand ourselves, how we interpret the world and how we treat others. From Genesis to the aboriginal songlines of Australia, human beings have forever perceived that naming brings the essence of things into being. . . . Words make worlds.
>
> Tippet 2016

Words take meaning from the private to the public domain, and in the first half of this book we wrote about how to do this in one-to-one and group settings. However, organisations are a public domain in which talking about meaning is both particularly important and particularly hard to do. The following case illustrates this.

Case Study 7.1 **Why is meaning so difficult to speak about in organisations?**

One practitioner was recently working with some very forward-thinking CEOs and managers of well-known mid-size and large-size organisations. 'I asked them if meaning was important in the workplace. On a scale of 0–10 with 10 as really important, they all placed it at 8 and above. The reasons they said it was important were:

- 'If something doesn't have meaning you are just filling in, or wasting, time.'
- 'We need a shared meaning or purpose, otherwise we can't pull together.'
- 'Meaning covers why we do things, doesn't it?'
- 'It gives you your direction, your purpose.'

When asked how easy it was to talk about they laughed and placed it between 0 and 1.5. Asked what created this huge gap they identified that:

- 'It never seems 'relevant' in a management meeting so it never gets on to the agenda.'
- 'The time it might take – we could be opening a can of worms. It's risky.'
- 'You can't put it on a spread-sheet.'
- 'It's personal and every person is different, so it feels overwhelming.'
- 'There's no end-point to it.'
- 'It all sounds too touchy-feely.'
- 'In some organisations it seems almost rude to ask 'Why are we all here each day?''
- 'There is little experience of this inquiry in organisations and very little shared definition or agreement.'
- 'Sometimes one-to-one is easier but often at board level and shareholder level it's seen as too 'soft' and not relevant to the bottom line.'
- 'Managers don't know how to include this need in their governance.'
- 'It's easier over a beer.'

The Map fills this gap, between knowing it is really important to talk about meaning and finding it difficult, unwieldy or scary in organisational contexts. The participants in the workshop left inspired with confidence that they could now address this gap because with the Map the conversation is more constructive (and hence not 'opening a can of worms'); it is structured (so less overwhelming and there is an endpoint to it); it is legitimised and concrete (so less 'touchy-feely'); it is more relevant, and it lends an element of practicality to the conversation (the Map is certainly no spreadsheet, but it is graphic, simple and people can easily place findings and solutions onto it).

While at one level, the above case study clearly shows why meaning is not talked about in organisations, paradoxically, employees speak about meaning all the time, often in negative ways. The can of worms that CEOs are so worried about opening is regularly opened in the world of experience of employees. It's just that this usually sounds like that endless litany of complaints, that so frustrate senior management, such as:

> Obviously Head Office has no idea of how it is for us out in the regions. If I try and implement this form with my clients, they'll just laugh in my face. It just gets completely in the way of my being actually able to help them [conflicts between two realities – Head Office and the Regions].

> If I raise my concerns once more about the ethical issues of the latest initiative, they're going to think I am a trouble-maker and I just don't know if I can risk it. But it breaks my heart to see what's happening to this organisation [challenges to Moral Growth].

> You'll never believe what they have just done. Broken up our team, and put half of us in another building. Honestly, I just don't know why I bother [destruction of Unity with Others].

> I gave them a great idea about what to do and no-one even responded. Well, that's the last time I do that [blocking Expressing Full Potential].

> I raised the ethical issues with this initiative, but they just gave me the old fish eye and went on as if I had never spoken. The previous boss was an upright type of bloke, but this one compromises our values without even realising it [ignoring issues to do with Integrity with Self].

> I explained that I came here to be with patients and that all I do is run around like a mad thing and when I sit down its only to stare at a computer. What difference will that ever make? [disconnection from Service to Others].

> We had this motivational speech from the Big Boss which was great, then three weeks later the budgets come out and all I am faced with is trying to achieve this great vision with a 10 per cent reduction in resources. I feel resentful, why promise a vision when we can't live up to it? [lack of constructive connection between Inspiration and Reality of Circumstances].

When you listen for meaning in this way, it is everywhere. But without the insights provided by the Map of Meaning, the yearning for meaning often sounds negative and disempowered, creating barriers of cynicism between management and staff.

Without a constructive language that enables us to powerfully speak about our human need for meaning, and without a framework which helps us to speak about meaning in ways that lead directly to action, we cannot design meaning into our organisations.

An additional problem is that in organisations a particular language is used that takes us away from meaning. It is a language that legitimises business or organisational outcomes and often silences human needs. This 'business' way of talking is dominant everywhere, be it in large commercial organisations, smaller units or not-for-profits, and these days even primary schools, sports clubs and community organisations. This makes it very hard to speak to human motivations and concerns.

It seems, for example, irrelevant or inappropriate, during an organisational change, to say, 'but I will miss my colleagues if our teams are reorganised this way' or 'but if I have two minutes less to complete the job, I no longer have time to ask the customer "how is your daughter, how did the operation go"', or 'but that means I have less time for what I really love which is teaching'. Such comments seem petty or inappropriately personal and self-focused when the organisation's survival is on the line. Or they seem unprofessional, as if we don't understand the real world of work.

And even if it is safe to say them, and they are met with a sympathetic glance, they do not seem to have the power that business words have. This is not just a problem for employees, it is a problem for the organisation, because it means it has few real ways of accessing the world of experience of those working for the organisation (including managers). As mentioned in Chapter 6, this world of experience is where employees are constantly judging what is meaningful and what is not and this judgement influences all desirable organisational outcomes such as creativity, teamwork, integrity, loyalty, and customer service.

Many people, when they hear this business jargon, feel disempowered because it removes them from what they know, and it often confuses the issue for them. Their hearts close down because what they hear seems removed from their real motivations and dehumanises their contributions. As early as 1905, Weber warned that organisations might end up with either specialist without spirit or sensualist without heart. With regard to the 'sensualist without heart' it has been suggested that language promoting love, compassion or authenticity is now artificially introduced into organisations to disguise the lack of spirit (Ritzenberg 2012). But this just exacerbates the inspiration-reality gap. Neither the managerialist nor sentimental language is natural to human beings, and in fact neither language is particularly grounded in experience, but language of meaning is.

The language of meaning is powerful because it is not an invented language with meaningless terms and jargon. It is a language that is natural to all members of the organisation in their everyday experience of life and work. It is a language in which all people can contribute, and express themselves, and therefore it reduces the impact of hierarchy. This language is simple and direct, though it can require courage, given the comments above, which is why it is so helpful to have the Map present because it normalises and legitimises this human expression. In using the Map, people become clear on what is really meant by goals, practices and decisions, what they mean the next day for everybody at work, and what has been agreed to and disagreed with in regard to the daily reality of work. It is this, involving everyone, that keeps meaning alive.

Keeping meaning alive

Because meaning is continuous and ever-changing, both within individuals and in response to circumstances, it is different from vision and mission and strategy. It can, as we saw in the previous chapter, inform all of these, but in the end meaning is shaped by the daily actions, decisions and practices that connect managers and employees to each other and to the overall purpose of the organisation. As we showed in Chapter 6, meaning takes place in the daily world of experience, and the absence and presence of it is tested day-to-day, week-to-week, month-to-month.

Keeping the mission and vision alive is of great concern to organisations, and there is abundant advice on how to do this such as 'tell everyone', 'have it on your website', 'have a daily alert on screens' or other techniques. While this can be useful, the real issue is not 'how do we keep the vision alive?' but 'how to keep managers and employees alive to the vision' and this seems impossible when, in the day-to-day experience of work, meaning is interrupted or destroyed. One of the problems, as mentioned by the CEOs, is that discussions about meaning, without the Map, can be time consuming. Meaning is often recognised when present or absent, but not easily volunteered in conversations.

Lisl Klein (2008), who spent over thirty years studying meaningful work, gives an account of interviewing someone in an organisation to understand his motivation. She found that listening to meaning required getting through different layers. He began with the obvious: 'All I'm interested in is the money. This firm pays well, and that's the only reason I stop here. What a working man wants from his job is the pay packet, and don't let anybody kid you about other fancy notions. Half an hour later he was talking about the firm: 'Well, you see, when you get a bit older, and the kids are off your hands, and you've paid for the house, and your wife's got a washing machine – you don't need the money so much anymore and you find you start noticing the firm. And by God it can annoy you!' Half an hour after that he said, 'You know – what I really like is when the machine goes wrong and I'm the only one knows how to put it right' (Klein 2008: 37–8).

She writes that, like the skins of an onion, a range of meanings exists in most people and the question is which of these gets tapped. The Map helps in quickly tapping this deeper layer of meaning and so supporting people to voice it. Doing this, Klein notes, is not a matter of being 'nice' to people. It is about being consistent:

> In terms of mental health, it seems to me to be dangerous and damaging that we express one set of values in our private, social, and political lives and a different set of values in our working arrangements, without really intending to. And we need to be more proactive in the way we design these things.
>
> Klein 2008: 260

To keep meaning alive, it needs to go beyond an externally imposed technique to an internal compass against which everything is checked. The Map is such a compass, which in simple language, breaks overall purposes down in doable pathways, so it can be embedded in planning and action.

We have noticed people being very inventive in keeping the Map of Meaning alive in their workplace. Many organisations put a copy of the Map in meeting rooms, so that they can listen for issues of meaningfulness and its loss. People use it to prepare for performance appraisals, to plan a new project, design new aspects of their job. Organisations can use the Map to question current practices, or behaviours. Where are employees collaborating? Where do people fudge answers? Virtually all examples that we have used in the previous chapters of the book are from people just finding a way to collectively keep meaning alive. We also noticed in previous chapters that 'keeping meaning alive' does not have to be driven from the top, and in fact is often not. Of course feelings are relevant because meaning (and particularly the lack of it) is felt deeply. However, with the Map, with the logic of an intellectually rigorous framework, the head and heart can be integrated in upward, downward and sideways organisational communication. This happens if everybody at all levels of the organisation is trusted to know what is meaningful for them.

Using meaningfulness as an ongoing part of organisational processes

In this case study we show how meaning, rather than being just a personal quest, becomes a natural part of decision making in an organisation using the Map.

Case Study 7.2 **Decision making in a commercial company**

This is a case study of a strategic decision-making group in a commercial organisation. This group had gone through a one-day training session on the Map and decided that they would keep the learning visible and actionable by putting a big poster of the Map in the meeting room.

It was quite unobtrusive there. However, during their meetings employees found themselves swinging around in their chairs pointing to various aspects of it. There is usually a lot on the agenda in these meetings so the board members tend to become quite business-like. The Map really assisted planning for the important basics, the things that matter most. When they talked about the extent to which they wanted to engage with the union and were well into a discussion about whether this would be efficient or inconvenient, someone pointed towards Unity with Others and said, 'What would the question look like from that perspective?' It shifted the decision-making process and later they worked very constructively with the union and have ever since. When restructuring came up someone asked, 'Could we consider restructuring with Expressing Full Potential in mind?' We could then easily discuss how each new position would need to facilitate skills development and that gained tremendous buy-in. When leasing a new fleet of cars it was noticed that in the quadrant of Service, the board had written: 'purchasing towards the future we want to create', so it was a small step to include a series of sustainability measures into the purchase plan. When the board looked at its own functioning it decided more Being time was required and started the meetings with a check-in and extended lunch time. Some of these things the board might have eventually arrived at as they match its vision and values, but others might have been completely overlooked or not have been handled so constructively, whereas the Map connected them so easily to all day-to-day decisions. The shape and structure of the Map, the words in it and its easy presence enable any group to efficiently and naturally integrate deeper questions into their decision-making.

Rosa writes that the accelerated pace of life and work often leads to individualisation, as the individual can accelerate more easily than the collective (Rosa 2013). As a result, the search for meaning often becomes an individualised concern and the quest for meaning is seen as separate from group decision making, meetings and planning. Yet, when the most important conversations are put on the backburner, meaning is often unintentionally diminished (Lips-Wiersma and Morris 2011; Amabile and Kramer 2012; Bailey and Madden 2016). By making the whole of meaningful work visible, groups can collectively cultivate it, as well as collectively protect against its disappearance, through collective responses to change initiatives, in strategic planning, or in a daily meeting.

Most processes used for strategic planning, such as a SWOT analysis, separate the person from the system. The planning happens 'out there' for the organisation as separate from 'in here' – that is, how we actually feel about not just the plan itself, but our own involvement as managers and employees in making this plan happen, starting tomorrow. In addition, when the divergent contributions of members of the organisation are easily heard within an organisational context, it allows 'soft' feelings to be included in 'hard' decisions in ways that bring dignity to the people and the process.

As one certified practitioner reflects, after using the Map of Meaning in numerous strategic planning sessions:

> I have worked in organisations right from the bottom to being the Manager of Operations, the second in command of a large not for profit. At present I help other organisations with their strategic planning. When I first saw the Map in a workshop it made complete intuitive sense to me. It instantly clicked and I could see its relevance to strategic planning, amongst other things, because it responds to the complexities, the multiple realities that you have to deal with in organisations: people, different personalities, competing priorities, organisational demands, financial realities. You are always trying to marry up so many different things. I sensed how the Map covered all of these, how it allowed us to look at all the dimensions and grasp this complexity and work with it, yet not feel overwhelmed.

Organisations often use a SWOT analysis for example, and this is fine, and has its uses, but it often misses the vision and purpose part. Then if you do the vision and purpose, the SWOT analysis does not always speak directly to that. So you get the bits, but not so clearly how they all interconnect, and certainly not how they interconnect in the fluid way required as an organisation responds to events and circumstances within itself and outside. The Map consistently shows us how all the dimensions are interrelated, so that we can keep this interaction in sight at all times.

And I am constantly amazed by how it is all covered by the Map. I spent an entire weekend going through all the strategic questions I had developed from the dimensions of the Map, and I checked them against all the questions that are usually asked, the areas that need to be covered in strategic planning. It was all there, but from such a different perspective. In one way I think it is because the entire process is grounded in the human need for meaning. So all the language comes from that, and that sits so well with people. It is why we have organisations, to do things that have meaning to people. When we use language that comes from something else (which you can see by asking people to draw an organisation. Many of them draw an organisational chart or a diagram. When we create a strategic plan from a diagram, naturally we don't get a workplace that feels alive with meaning), we instantly separate people from their intrinsic motivation and that is madness really, because that is the one thing we desperately need, both as people working in organisations and in organisations as entities. And coming from meaning also consistently results in people eager to take action, to take responsibility. They are longing to fulfil the vision, the purpose of the organisation. What we have been waiting for is a way to easily and holistically do this. And it works well, because it is based in what people already know, in their experience. And so deep feelings can be expressed but in ways that are easily heard within an organisational context, allowing 'soft' feelings to be included in 'hard' decisions in ways that bring dignity to the people and the process.

Speaking and designing for meaning at an organisational level

Having a legitimised language of meaning allows us to reclaim organisations as the creation of human beings, and therefore subject to us, rather than the other way around. This is, in itself, empowering. 'This is so simple, and so overwhelming in its consequences', was the response of one workshop participant upon recognising that an organisation can be designed in a multitude of ways. Putting the human need for meaning at the foundation of our thinking helps us to rethink the way we conceptualise organisations.

We can already see this in the way that the increase in the service sector over the past decades has altered the nature of organisations, encouraging flatter structures and more flexibility. Or in the rise of social entrepreneurs and the inventiveness with which they are designing new ways of working. While no large-scale organisations have been designed on the basis of the Map of Meaning, some smaller ones have, and that is because in such organisations people often organise naturally. However, even within the context of a smaller organisation, we have found it is important to use the Map to articulate what comes naturally. There is a fine line between what is natural and what is subconscious, and when something is subconscious, it can easily be managed out. In the next two case studies we show why meaning requires constant articulation.

Case Study 7.3 **Designing meaningful work is natural**

I was asked to share the Map of Meaning with a local organisation that had been set up by women who had been to prison. Its mission was to support local women in prison and to support them and others in a way that would reduce the likelihood of returning to prison.

I was aware that I needed to learn more about their experience before I shared the Map with them. So I asked to sit in on a meeting and just observe. What I noticed was deeply moving. When I met with them again I said, 'I really cannot teach you anything. What I can do is mirror back to you your own deep wisdom'. I then shared the Map of Meaning with them, using examples of what they were already doing to show how they had intrinsically understood what was meaningful to them and embedded it in their organisation.

- **Inspiration**: The organisation was set up to provide a way to support women with prison experience and it did.

- **Unity with Others:** Each person during the meeting had mentioned how vital being in the group was to their well-being and their ability to stay out of prison. They shared stories and experiences, they were understood, they belonged.

- **Service to Others:** They were running a food bank to support other vulnerable families.

- **Expressing Full Potential:** Each of the women spoke about personal development and the skills training they were undertaking and their concern to be skilful in their roles.

- **Integrity with Self:** Each person spoke of the challenge of going straight, of keeping to what they knew was important to them, often in challenging circumstance.

- **Reality:** The inspiration had led to the creation of the group, and they were all totally realistic about the challenges they faced.

I was left feeling very humble in the face of their courage, dignity, honesty and passion. And by the fact that they already were acting from their own deep knowing of what was meaningful to them.

In the above case study, all elements of meaning get addressed in the organisation, from the bottom up. But organisations grow and meanings change, so how are meanings, once created, protected, and what is the role of speaking about meaning in this? In the final case study of this chapter we show that meaning cannot be protected when it cannot be made visible. As a result it is often 'managed out'. This is not only very frustrating to those who had meaning, but also very costly, as it means new managers can destroy meaning very quickly. The Managing Director who speaks in this case study has since started to use the Map of Meaning. He immediately recognised that it gave a framework for what he previously did 'because it made sense to him'. When we look at his actions they are all expressions of dimensions of the Map of Meaning. In four years he turned the company around with nearly a 50 per cent increase in productivity and a 75 per cent increase in profitability and left it positioned to be 'the best of its kind in the world'.

Case Study 7.4 **When meaningful work seems just like good business practice**

The Managing Director inherited an organisation that had a culture of blame, and where there was a somewhat gloomy business outlook.

'Volumes were declining, profits were not promising and customer service was at a low level resulting in increasing complaints and reduced loyalty from customers. The organisational structure was hierarchical, where the previous Managing Director led by abdication and second line management led by fear'. Not surprisingly, the personnel were largely dispirited. In undertaking what was a major transformation of the organisation, the MD focused on a series of changes to both culture and process, with the fundamental drive to move an organisation that was hierarchical into one where people took more personal responsibility. This met with resistance from the Management Team, and led finally to two positions being made redundant.

'Directly after taking away the two main management positions, I encouraged, coached and trained all the remaining staff in their work and personal development. During the first year I had become convinced of their knowledge and experience, but they themselves had to start believing in it as well. This structural change became the basis for the new team, the new organisation and the new culture. Most of the staff stepped up their game instantly. It required time for some others, but within one year nearly all the staff embraced the new culture, believed in the company and in themselves and they started to enjoy the increased responsibilities.

The MD worked on improving relationships with customers, both strengthening existing ones and developing new ones, changing the office layout to better support the new open, direct culture, and creating a warmer receptive environment for other stakeholders.

The final stage was to implement the new culture among the warehouse staff. One aspect of this was to involve the Union from the beginning, including them in plans and decisions involving some redundancies. As a result the 'process went very smoothly and within a couple of weeks everything was completed'.

All this change was supported by new and/or revised systems and processes. A vacant office was set up as a gym, another as a canteen and a number of mess rooms were reduced to one so that all staff could gather together.

Within four years this culture and process change was largely complete and the results justified the changes, supported by a strong team spirit, clear job descriptions, regular feedback throughout the organisation, respectful relationships, vastly improved customer relations and a good relationship with the Unions'.

At the beginning of this case study it is easy to see that there is no Unity among any layer of the organisation, including the line managers. No-one was taking responsibility, but blaming others, excusing themselves and retreating into denial. This detachment from Reality was creating an unprosperous future with increasing customer complaints indicating no real Service to Others and, therefore, no Inspiration.

There was little personal challenge for employees, so little chance for them to Express their full potential. Within this situation people were unhappy and felt a need to mask themselves and to pretend, which often happens in the face of fear. As a result people were moving away from Integrity with Self, as their energy was directed into suppression and survival.

The new MD looked the Reality squarely in the face – the current state of the organisation and its future prospects. He then began with Inspiration, a vision of what he wanted to accomplish. This was largely focused on repairing relationships – Unity with Others – through renegotiating the labour contract, and the relationships with stakeholders and staff. He then concentrated on developing all staff: both assisting them to express full potential and to increase their ability to have integrity with self through coaching as well as training – focusing on examining questions around 'who am I being?' as well as building skills. Staff began to believe in themselves as a result. Relationships across the board began to improve and new ones were created. Unity was further strengthened through actions that included reorganising the office space and installing open counters to facilitate connection with the lorry drivers.

This was then followed up with a full culture change, again stressing Unity by involving the unions from the beginning.

Unfortunately, with a new manager stepping in, a lot of the positive changes were lost, and this in turn negatively affected productivity and profitability. So, what went wrong?

These days management changes so rapidly that it is important to make visible (in more than economic terms) what a manager contributes, particularly, how they contribute to creating a meaningful workplace, so that the lessons can be handed on.

Without the legitimisation and distinctions that a recognised language gives us about the significance of meaningful work, every step can be dismantled. There are many good managers, but the effects of their role are often only described in terms of business language, such as business growth and employee and customer satisfaction. This does not capture the processes, or the world of experience between the purpose and the systems world that they influence.

Unless the essence of manager's work, that is how they created meaning, can be mapped, be part of the feedback process or otherwise captured in language, this meaning can easily (and often unintentionally) be destroyed, particularly when the manager does not ensure his or her workforce take on (protect and become responsible for) the language of meaning.

To end with a positive example: one certified practitioner used the Map as a way to frame a two-day strategic planning workshop. At the end of the two days the team was completely energised and had identified many practical ways forward. At the end of the workshop, the CEO, who had not been present, took fifteen minutes to give his view of things in business language and nearly destroyed everything that had been accomplished, leading to further destruction of not only morale but also of training investment. How often have we experienced something similar?

In this case the group could stand strong in their newly claimed language of meaning and as a result distinguish their plans from 'business as usual' and, also because their language was constructive, get the CEO on board.

Summary

- Research has established most of what needs to be known about creating meaningful work and avoiding meaningless work. What is not well know is how to move organisations from what is technically and theoretically known, to what is actually done in practice. To bridge this gap it is vital for everybody in the organisation to have words to speak about what matters most.

- When people at all levels of the organisation give a score of ten to the importance of talking about meaning and a two to their ability to do so, there is a problem. Organising is communicating and communicating is organising, so if meaning cannot be communicated it cannot be included in organising.

- Organisations are fast paced; it is therefore not possible to take hours to unravel a person's personal meaning. Yet if the individual does not uncover what is personally meaningful, their contribution to dialogue about organisational meaning is likely to be cynical or suppressed. The Map, because it can operate at both individual and organisational level, is very effective in communicating meaning.

- Once it is clear what is meaningful, it is important to keep sight of it, in both daily work and decisions, as well as at CEO and strategic level. Simply having the Map physically present helps us speak about meaning in a confident and effective way.

- In breaking down what creates and destroys meaning, and connecting it to particular actions, it becomes concrete and manageable. That means it cannot be destroyed so easily when the next idea or the next manager comes along. Meaningful work that fulfils the purpose of the organisation is now everyone's responsibility.

- Meaning is easy to introduce into a conversation, a presentation or a strategic plan when you use the Map, and leads to instant recognition and deep comprehension. Employees, teams and managers can hold the Map in their minds or put it up in various places at work and so easily bring it into daily activities. It is not intrusive, it does not conflict with dearly held world-views and it helps people engage with and act on human issues. Because it is grounded and practical it can be used in ways that energise people so they can put talk into immediate action.

8

Meaningful work through integrated systems

In chapters five and six we explained that the different dimensions of meaningful work are in a dynamic relationship with each other. When one dimension, such as Unity is expressed too much, especially over a period of time and at the exclusion of others, a loss of meaning occurs. This also explains how a job or vocation that was initially experienced as very meaningful might lose its meaning over time. Or why a job that is full of meaning to one person may not be experienced as so meaningful by others.

The following story is from a practitioner who applies the Map to sustainability work. One of the employees of the organisation she was working with said: 'The sustainability focus of my organisation has given me great opportunities to develop my talents, and I ended up designing a waste system for camper vans in my city. As we attract thousands of campervans a year, this is really making a difference, and I also now feel much better about working here as I feel I am living my values. But I am still not getting it right because the cleaners hate having to separate out the rubbish as it takes up so much of their time'.

The practitioner showed the employee that she was doing what naturally led to meaningful work to her. She was helping the environment, using her talents, and aligning her values with her work. All that was missing was the Unity dimension of meaning, which was to work with the cleaners so that they too could find their work meaningful. From just this simple conversation, the employee had a much clearer sense of what she needed to do next, and why it was important to her and the cleaners to address this issue so that the Unity aspect of her initiative could be strong.

In Chapter 6 we discussed speaking about meaning in an organisational context and that this takes place in the space of human experience between the organisational purpose and systems. In this chapter, we look at integrating all dimensions of meaning into the systems. We will look at a performance review and a recruitment exercise to show how, when the dimensions of meaning can be expressed at the same time, they strengthen each other and the individual experiences the system as having a sense of wholeness or inner order.

Integrated organisational practice

In the world of purpose, it is clear what the organisation is for and every-body in the organisation needs to 'own' the purpose statement. The world of human experience, on the other hand, is where conversations take place and emotions and energy (or lack of it) are felt. If we consider the systems as a whole from the perspective of the employee, techniques and practices are created that either confirm that work does have meaning, or (often unintentionally) convey the message that work has no meaning.

One good example is the performance appraisal. Potentially these can be a useful time for evaluating where one has been, where one is going and how this fits with the purpose of the organisation. Indeed, HR managers might argue that they are critical to personal and organisational success.

A quick Internet search will show that over time there have been many efforts to perfect the technique. Currently there are at least 11 groups of tried and tested techniques (e.g. behaviourally anchored scales, critical incident methods, management by objectives) on the market; each group carries a wide range of tests one can choose from.

A quick search will also reveal that performance appraisals often com-pletely miss the target. One website summarises: they're every manager's yearly conundrum. In theory, performance reviews make sense. In practice, the exercise borders on the absurd: you have one hour to review a whole year's worth of work, issue a grade usually based on a rudimentary 'satisfaction' scale, and outline goals that you likely won't revisit until next year's meeting (Korosec 2010).

Korosec goes on to say how the performance review has become a mere 'jumping through the HR hoop'. To find a solution to this problem, each of the websites that identifies problems aims to fix them by adding another technique. Some of these techniques are undoubtedly quite useful: for example, talking less and asking more questions, or having more organic ongoing reviews rather than annual events. But few ask, 'if we are all doing them, how can we organise them so they can become an integrated and constructive experience, rather than a fragmented and demotivating one?'; 'Who do we need to have in the room to design them as a meaningful experience'; 'What questions give management feedback on the extent to which work is actually perceived to be meaningful in practice'?

One general manager, using the Map of Meaning, did ask these questions and redesigned his organisation's performance reviews to make them a more meaningful process (Case Study 8.1).

Case Study 8.1 Using the Map as a basis for redesigning performance appraisal

The general manager (GM), who has known about the Map for many years, decided to use it as the basis for rethinking performance design in his organisation.

The GM had never enjoyed the process of Performance Appraisal; the rating of people, the sense of being judged and judging, and the limited focus of the questions. He saw it as neither productive, in that it never led to changes in the organisational systems or culture, nor as meaningful for most of the people going through the process.

Using the questions in Chapter 2, he designed questions that captured the essence of each dimension of meaning, from the employee's point of view. When he mapped these questions against what he needed to know to create a well-functioning organisation, he found the questions covered the whole. For example, he needed to know how the team was functioning and how the individual was functioning in the team, as well as their perception of the organisational culture. He found that the questions under 'Unity', such as 'do you experience mutual support in your relationships at work?; Can you talk about what deeply matters to you?; Do you feel at home or out of place at work?' covered these.

He then tried out the new performance review with the senior management team and sought their feedback on it. Their responses were overwhelmingly positive, with individuals repeatedly pointing to how the process had enabled an honest and deeper understanding of self, others and professional role. Collectively, the management team commented on how using the Map had enabled the review process to develop into a relaxed and 'human' exchange, compared to the 'rigid, boring experience of previous Performance Appraisals'. In addition they had suggestions to make about what other questions could capture their experience and how they could collectively act on some of the themes that emerged from the review.

In reflecting on the experience, the GM found that designing the performance review on the basis of the Map worked, for three reasons:

- Performance reviews often focus on one area, such as developing skills, or career opportunities sought by the employee. By using the Map the GM felt confident that all basics were covered. With questions about all dimensions of meaningful work, the review provided the GM with much richer information about the whole person and all aspects of their work. Employees spoke about their experience not just in relation to themselves as an individual employee but also in relation to the system as a whole. They spoke to Self and Other, to Being and Doing. This gave the GM much more accurate feedback on what to keep and treasure and what to change or let go.

- The human language of meaning meant that people responded differently. Everybody, including the GM, spoke more clearly and more practically.

- Performance reviews, without intending to do so, trigger a whole parent–child dynamic in the world of experience. Someone is in power and has all the right questions to ask, and the other person just gets to answer them. The process of co-creating and seeking feedback on the techniques avoids fragmentation. At the same time, the structure of the Map encourages thoughtful input and is not unwieldy.

From the perspective of the GM, he now has a process that completely integrates purpose, experience and system techniques:

> The performance review confirms that their inspiration aligns with that of the organization. They speak from a place that acknowledges that our work is really worthwhile and that they have a sense of belonging, of being part of a strong family, and that through their work they grow as people. It was revealing to them and to me to explore this depth of connection to the purpose of the work, rather than just focusing on their tasks. This is showing up now in a number of ways. When we have our monthly meeting, it now occurs in a different context, one in which we are all inspired and the tasks are an expression of that.

The GM also found that in using all the dimensions of the Map he was able to get to the heart of those elements of the system that were getting in the way of meaningfulness, and where and if the organisation had lost its balance.

> People are very happy not having to rate themselves – instead, I learn about them in terms of a potential vulnerability they have, rather than a weakness. I find the process more intuitive – for example, one individual was a little out of balance in her Being, and this showed itself in her time management, but what I am impressed by is that she saw this herself and arrived at her own solution through the review.

Having enjoyed and identified with the process, the management team expressed excitement at the prospect of working through the questions with their own teams. For both those involved and the practitioner it was very inspiring to see how an existing and potentially valuable process can be revitalised by framing it from a more holistic perspective.

When the Map is used to diagnose the problem, the solutions to the problem also address all dimensions of the Map. The Map does not prescribe specific solutions for each dimension. This leads to more innovation as we can see through the next case study on recruitment. The certified practitioner used the Map in a number of ways during a team building day for a recruitment brand team.

Case Study 8.2 **Enriching recruitment**

The recruitment team spanned four different countries and once a year they came together over three days to bond as a team and review strategy. My brief was to host the first day as a fun team-building day that could also feed into the strategy day by having a 'future focus'. Given their geographical split, there was a strong 'us and them' mentality. This would be the first time many were meeting face to face, as many of the younger people in the team were new. The age of participants ranged widely between early twenties and early sixties. I used the Map of Meaning as an 'umbrella' framework for the day, exploring the question 'what is meaningful work?' at an individual, team and organisational/societal level. The first step was to explore participants' individual sense of meaningful work by creating visual collages of the Map.

They then shared these with each other, generating powerful insights. They observed that despite their generational and geographical differences they shared similar values. They said that they got to know each other better in an hour than they had on previous team building days doing cooking lessons or sporting activities together! They learned new things and surprising things about each other, that enabled them to see each other in a new light. For example, one older participant spoke of his active involvement in his local church, something he had never discussed at work. He was anxious about sharing it, but his commitment to helping his local community created a huge respect for him, and enabled his colleagues to see him in a different way – as a whole person. You could feel an opening happening; it bridged cultural barriers and also generational barriers.

The second step was to explore how the team were currently experiencing meaning or lack of meaning at work, through an exercise walking through a large Map of Meaning on the floor. Given that the team leaders were also in the exercise, this enabled a very constructive dialogue around what was working well and what people needed more of in order to experience more meaning. One key insight was that in order to contribute to their full potential at work the team wanted more sight and understanding of the company's future strategic direction from their leaders.

The third step of the day was to explore what the future of work looked like through video footage and other future search exercises. From there, participants were asked to create and act out a three minute 'company recruitment video of the future' for their company. They were asked to refer to the four pathways of the Map of Meaning as a way to structure the video. Some really interesting sketches emerged including, for example, a prospective employee interviewing the company's Chief Happiness Officer. In another video they illustrated the ways the company helped employees develop their inner-self (e.g. mindfulness at work, flexible working) and be of service to others through their sustainability strategy. These were quite a departure for a very conservative company in an industry sector seriously challenged by sustainability. Essentially they saw that it was important to speak to all four pathways of meaning in their recruitment communications to create an attractive offer in the future workplace. Following this exercise they were keen to put their existing communications through the 'Map of Meaning test' to identify what messages they were missing. The team leader also wanted to explore how the Map of Meaning could inform their recruitment positioning in relation to recruitment.

The client evaluation forms showed that the day had supported their strategy day and, compared to other team boosters, this day had been more useful and more enjoyable, more personal and meaningful, and had led to new thinking in terms of how they recruited their staff.

Through this intervention I observed that by working with the Map of Meaning in layers (individual, team, organisational, societal) we can bridge the divides between self and others, and between our work and our impact the world. All this as part of a fun team building day!

While a completely different context from the performance case study, there are parallels in that the Map connects the personal world of experiencing meaning to the organisational purpose. In addition, through attending to all dimensions of the Map, the particular output (in this case a recruitment video) is not only more complete but immediately practical in that it changed how the organisation now recruits staff.

It is also interesting to see in this case study how effortlessly the Map of Meaning provides a simple way to integrate and unify aspects of the organisation (in this case, communication), and that the staff themselves immediately wanted to use it to evaluate all their other communication products. If they did, it would generate a coherent and unified communication strategy, and one that was inherently meaningful.

What is interesting to note in both case studies is that in collectively working with the Map the team connects at a profound level. Both cases show that through the Map, practices that can otherwise be experienced as quite separate from each other (team building, purposing, designing a technique for recruitment) now have a natural flow and connection.

Balancing meaningful tasks through job crafting

We first introduced ideas of wholeness and integration in Chapter 4. There we also introduced unmitigated expressions of meaningful work, where one or more dimensions were expressed to the exclusion of others. Unmitigated development of the inner self became 'self-absorption'; of serving others became 'sacrifice'; of unity 'subsuming self'; and of expressing full potential 'self oriented goal striving'. But what is the role of organisations in creating such unbalanced work experiences, ones that diminish meaning?

In organisations it often becomes obvious that 'things have gone too far'. But it is hard for people to find the language, beyond complaining about work pressure in general, to compellingly identify what is really going on and when they and the organisation truly are in danger, so that they can be heard by those in power. Most of the time, when there is imbalance, Service to Others is expressed at the exclusion of the other dimensions of meaningful work. One person in our UK workshops who works in the health service noticed how the extreme pressure to serve others, with virtually no time for Self, had led to examples of patient abuse. 'It's as if they have gone to the very opposite of what they came to do as nurses. They came to care for people and now they are so stressed themselves that they are careless and rude'.

Stereotypically, not-for-profits are pushing too much sacrifice; a church might push too much conformity so that unique identities become subsumed into others; a bank might push too much selfish goal striving. These are indeed stereotypes, but examples of organisations going out of balance usually take place at more subtle levels and the Map helps to recognise and address this before it is too late and extreme expressions of meaning become embedded in the culture and structure of the organisations.

The following case study is from a certified practitioner who uses the Map in organisations to notice and address imbalances. When an employee has the ability to recraft their job, and their line-manager is supportive of this, they can often reshape their roles and task to obtain more balance. While this is not possible in many organisations, there are often more opportunities for job crafting than employees (particularly overwhelmed employees) assume.

Case Study 8.3 **On time management**

My rationale for using the Map in this context is that it addresses a need that I regularly come across: the need for people to be able to see their work as more than just a process of 'delivering the goods' or 'meeting the targets' (both are terms I use for Service to Others). I have reached this conclusion because I noticed that people who are heavily focused on production, delivery, processing – those who are very 'doing oriented' – can become distant, depressed and disillusioned with their work. They sense a lack of purpose despite being very busy and while they know something is not right they see getting busier as the solution to their problem. From my observations, getting busier is the last thing they need, because their work and life has already become imbalanced to the extent, in some cases, of showing early stages of 'workaholism'.

This situation is exacerbated in many organisations because key performance indicators have been, and often still are, very focused on the achievement of goals, many of which are externally driven. Achievement of these goals in this particular organisation, while giving a sense of 'making a difference', came at the expense of the three other pathways to meaningful work: development of either self or team, building and maintaining relationships, and expressing their full potential in a way that their talents are freely flowing.

An example involves a man in his early thirties who was managing the IT help desk for a large organisation. By definition this job was a highly delivery-based Service to Others as it was almost solely based on receiving and responding to customer calls. The manager was effectively running a call centre and carried out a task that could never be completed. He had become totally focused on 'delivering the goods' and it quickly became apparent that he was suffering from minor depression. His work was suffering, his relationships with family and colleagues were suffering, he was getting more and more frustrated and as a result he was doing his job less and less well.

I drew a cross on a piece of paper, named each of the four quadrants of the Map, then asked him to indicate approximate percentages of how he was spending his time. The division was 90–95 per cent of the time in 'delivering the goods' with the remaining 5–10 per cent being split between the other three quadrants. It very quickly made visible that he was using his time in a seriously unbalanced way and was also missing out on the range of activities necessary to sustain a healthy life.

We began by looking at how to approach the problem from the perspective of Unity. He decided that he needed more unity with his clients. We built an action plan to help him create good relationships with his clients beyond just helping them when they had a problem. He decided to meet his clients in person around a number of themes where they reported the most problems. He met them individually and in groups and introduced not only himself but also his team to them. This also meant that the callers weren't just dealing with faceless scape-goats when they dialled in and stopped taking out their frustrations on call centre employees. By doing this, he was also increasing 'integrity with self', by learning to stand strong, with the help of others, to do the job that was actually being asked of him.

There were three consequences to his actions. First, his health, attitude and sense of purpose improved immediately and he regained a sense of being in charge of himself; second, the number of calls dropped and third, the nature of these calls changed from being frustrated and unfriendly to being cheerful and friendly. The calls became a 'request for help' rather than 'blaming for the problem'. Obviously this made a huge difference to everyone involved.

Designing a balanced organisation

Organisations are designed and populated by people. People are driven by the search for meaning. The organisations in which they work need a way to be coherent and to make sense of competing needs. However, unless organisational design reflects who we are as human beings, fragmentation and splitting inadvertently shapes much of organisational life. This alienates people from their personal purpose, distances them from the organisational purpose, locks them in silos and leads to competing priorities. Fragmented organisational designs also lead to internal dichotomies such as those at the top versus those at the bottom, those in marketing versus those in engineering, or external dichotomies such as the board versus the union.

Such fragmentation, in addition to an increasingly frantic pace of work and life, often results in a sense of overwhelming complexity. Where do we start when we want to change things? How do we hold on to what we value? What are the real levers in a system and how do we stay inspired when all our efforts get reorganised away in yet another round of change or cuts?

As we saw in the previous chapters, a vital aspect of the human need for meaning is met by a sense of coherence which comes from balancing Self and Other, Being and Doing, as well as Inspiration and Reality. This is a natural balance that each person seeks.

At an organisational level too, all four dimensions of the Map need to be consistently attended to. Imbalance, where one polarity is taken to an extreme, can make a mockery of the very purpose for which the organisation was established and of the commitment of its staff.

It is therefore important that we understand the organisational conditions that lead to balanced meaning, and those that lead to unmitigated expression of only one or two dimensions of meaning.

It makes perfect sense that a meaningful working life is a well-integrated or coherent working life and that organisations contribute to the extent a person can experience all meanings or are excessively pulled towards one meaning. However, there is little academic research on these ideas. There is research on burn-out and overwork, but this usually looks at a lack of personal or organisational resources. Doing more with less is not a problem that the Map can resolve, but the Map does help in identifying when organisational design is not whole, as we can see from the examples above.

Several authors have started to identify unmitigated expressions of the four dimensions of meaningful work:

- Bailey and Madden (2016), researching (among other occupations) solicitors, found that while solicitors experienced meaning from belonging to their particular professional group, they also experienced meaninglessness through too much emphasis on belonging: 'they want you to essentially behave like they do'.

- In relation to Integrity with Self, Schwartz and Sharp (2006) argued that too much of a virtue (e.g. assertiveness, or excellence) might be equally as harmful as too little. Yet such virtues can be balanced with other virtues such as kindness, or acceptance.

- Von Bergen, Campbell and Leard (2016: 149) give the example of a person valued for their creativity and out-of-the box thinking but who also avoided collaboration. Such a person would experience high meaning in 'expressing full potential' but low meanings in 'unity with others' and possibly in 'developing inner self'.

- An excess of contributing can lead to paternalism or imposing control (Berkelaar and Buzzanell 2015), in which case a person would no longer have 'unity with others'.

- Humle (2014), in relation to consultancy work, found research partici-pants reflected on the tensions between doing enough tasks to make a difference to a large enough group of people (Service to Others) and wanting each piece of work to be of high quality (Expressing Full Potential).

- In relation to academic life Vostal (2015) found it was important for an academic to balance too much time to think – which leads to passivity, motionlessness, procrastinating or excessive rethinking – with regularly expressing ideas that can start to make a difference.

- An example of being subsumed in others would be the research participant who, as a member of the Salvation Army, had lost his unique voice and identity (Lips-Wiersma 1999) and subsequently, as he realised this, changed his career but not until he had experienced burn out.

- Pavlish and Hunt (2012) show that, against the background of time acceleration, social relationships (Unity) suffer as workload (Service to Others) increases.

In some of this research, participants refer directly to the loss of meaning as a result of loss of balance 'when you run around and get caught up in . . . tasks and you step away from patients. It is hard to find meaning in that' (Pavlish and Hunt 2012: 119).

In this context, our multidimensional conceptualisation of meaningful work assists organisations to more deliberately design tasks so that individuals can experience all dimensions. For example, Bailey and Madden (2015) found that refuse collectors, who already experienced meaning through serving others, experienced additional meaning when they were given the opportunity to control the pace and timing of their own work, free from managerial controls. They now also experienced a sense of accomplishment (Expressing Full Potential): 'I was working out where I've got to be and in what order and it worked first time'.

While we could find little theory on what organisational designs that support multiple meanings in a balanced manner might look like, we found some conceptual ideas about how to think about designing organisations to avoid imbalance.

- Littleton, Arthur and Rousseau (2000) suggest that agency provides direction and diffuses ambiguity in organisations, but can also cause the formation of strong formal or informal hierarchies inhibiting meaningful career experiences. They suggest organisations need to be designed so that people can experience both personal initiative and mutual co-operation, an argument also made by Blustein (2011).

- Kahn (2001), in the context of care organisations, talks about 'holding environments' as places where people feel safe to express their true selves (Integrity with Self) so as to not lose themselves in caring for others (Serving Others).

- Goodpaster (2007) discusses the importance of creating spaces for ethical discernment to counterbalance the goal-drivenness of many organisations.

- Lindstrom (2016), doing research on meaningful work in a municipal setting, writes: 'the interviewees portrayed recognising the results of one's work [i.e. contributing to the well-being of the residents of the municipality]. However, there is no talk of day-to-day work itself as a source of meaningfulness, which results in a very goal-oriented view of meaningful work' (p. 194).

- It has been found that burnout as a result of too much caring cannot only be avoided by doing less caring but also by balancing the caring role with more agentic tasks (Expressing Full Potential) (Llorens *et al.* 2007). In this context the research on burn-out might give some interesting insights into the need for and effects of balancing multiple dimensions of meaningful work.

The importance of recognising Being in organisational design

In creating organisational designs against a background of the accelerating pace of work, it is particularly important to make the 'being' dimension of meaningful work visible.

Lack of time to attend to one's own needs, as well as lack of time to attend to work relationships, constrains the extent to which people take collective action and speak up (Expressing Full Potential), as found by Qin *et al.* (2014).

Darley and Batson (1973) found that time pressure greatly reduces prosocial behavior and that individuals who spend all their time 'doing' tend to focus on their own rather than the other person's needs. Since the main goal of busy individuals is to reduce time constraints, they pay little attention to other elements, such as co-workers or customers in need of help.

- With regard to 'integrity with self', Lips-Wiersma (2006) in research on organisational retreats found that where employees were given time within working hours to, in a structured manner, reflect on what was meaningful to them (rather than consider organisational goals), this self-reflection opportunity resulted in participants recrafting aspects of their work. What was particularly interesting to note in this study was that individual workers had had the freedom to engage in job crafting all along. However, it was not until they had structured time to think and feel what mattered to them that they recrafted aspects of their roles.

- Noonan (2009) found that, when they were able to reflect on what was the right thing to do, individuals balanced 'expressing full potential' with 'integrity with self' because they became aware of the different feelings that different causes of action evoked (e.g. anxiety, openness).

- More recently, organisation-level practices have emerged that are designed to cultivate 'being' such as organisational mindfulness (Weick and Sutcliffe 2006; Jordan *et al.* 2009;) and creating a reflective culture (Vince 2002).

This organisation-level literature is promising for cultivating the 'being' dimensions of meaningful work. It critiques overly individualist approaches to time management and relates the need for 'being' not only to personal well-being but also to individual agency, improved decision quality, ethics, service to others and creativity.

The importance of holistic thinking

As the arrows in the Map indicate, tensions between Being and Doing, Self and Other, are a natural part of our work and life. They are complex, but they don't have to become dysfunctional so we need to learn to see, hold and address the tensions. When the whole is in view this brings peace into the room. As stated by Skolimowski (1994: 141): 'thus wholeness is not only a descriptive term showing how parts are united within a pattern. It is also an epistemological term. Wholeness and holistic thinking are modes of understanding'. Seeing the whole gives everyone in an organisation powerful ways to make sense of what is happening, and leads to a range of practical and doable solutions.

Lisl Klein (2008: 174) argues that it is this ability to work with tensions that is 'the foundation of organisational learning'. We become skilful not only in seeing the whole, but in developing processes for working with the opposing forces. This is an insight picked up by many people working with the Map of Meaning that, by working with a limited number of apparently opposing issues, they are forced to create new, innovative and surprising solutions.

Summary

- At present, the techniques and practices used in the organisational system, with the aim of achieving the organisational purpose, seldom take multiple dimensions of meaning into account. This results in fragmentation and loss of coherence.

- In this chapter we showed that managers, consultants and trainers can redesign practices such as a performance review, recruitment, team building and job crafting by using all dimensions of the Map of Meaning.

- As a result, those experiencing the system found increased meaning in the practice, and more understanding of how they could continue to find or create meaning in the practice in the years to come.

- Meaning is not yet used as a framework to design organisations as a whole to support the balancing of the different dimensions. But several conceptual ideas are emerging on how to design so that Being and Doing, as well as Self and Other, are in balance in work and organisations.

9

Meaningful work at the foundation of the responsibility revolution

Never before has there been such a need for organisations to behave responsibly. While we see the emergence of green, participative and healthy initiatives, we are also painfully aware of the challenges posed by unravelling social cohesion and the degraded condition of the planet. What organisations do will significantly impact future generations. The effectiveness of their response, whether they are for-profit, not-for-profit or community organisations, is an expression of the way in which each one comes together and organises.

> The logic is simple: There is not one item on the global agenda for change that can be understood (much less responded to) without a better understanding of organisations. More than anywhere else, the world's direction and future are being created in the context of human organisations and institutions. Today . . . new spaces have opened for transboundary corporations, networks, nongovernmental organisations (NGOs), regimes, associations, grassroots groups and many others to proliferate. The significance, in many respects, of the relatively small number of decisions made by our nation-state leaders pales in comparison to the billions of decisions made every day by members and leaders of such organisations.
>
> Cooperrider and Dutton 1999: xvi

However, for too many employees the main mode of operation is one of 'muddling through' or 'fighting back', and there is widespread evidence of a shared and pervasive uneasiness in our experience of our daily working life (Scharmer 2007).

At the beginning of this book, we wrote that we cannot change organisations for the better without a profound understanding of what it is to be human. To be human is to search for meaning, to be energised by what is meaningful, and to long to have our actions firmly grounded in that which has meaning for ourselves and others.

At a time when existing organisations are taking on new responsibilities, when new enterprises are being created to specifically address social and environmental ills, and when organisations are taking on new forms and new alliances, there exists a truly radical and creative moment in which we can also re-examine and redefine work itself.

At the same time, there is a distinct danger that old and defunct organisational practices will be brought to bear on new organisational responsibilities. When we attend forums on sustainability and responsibility we notice how, in the need to be heard and taken seriously, there is much talk about technology, consumer buy-in and efficiency gains and still relatively little talk about how to engage the members of the organisations who, collectively, make the billions of decisions that result in responsible and sustainable organisations. We fear that when old ways of organising are brought to new organisational challenges, the change that will take place will not be sufficiently fundamental. We also fear that old patterns and habits will cripple an organisation's ability to respond as fully and successfully as its members might long to do.

There is an enormous opportunity to redesign work and organisations to better address the demands of the responsibility revolution. But, in order to do so, we believe we must rethink the very patterns of human purpose and interaction that constitute the modern organisation. We suggest that the Map of Meaning is fundamental to this because it demands that the question of what is a worthwhile life is given a significant place in the design of the organisations of the future.

In this chapter we focus on how working with the Map of Meaning integrates the need for meaningful work with socially and environmentally responsible organisational practices. As mentioned in the introduction to the book, the search for meaning is not just another fad; it is a fundamental aspect of the human condition, of human strength and well-being and is the foundation of choices that sustain our humanity. It is, therefore, fundamental to the responsibility revolution.

Responsible work holds great promise for employee commitment. An organisation 'is far more likely to win extraordinary contributions from people when they feel they are working toward a goal of extraordinary consequence' (Hollender and Breen 2010: 25). Such a statement (which we see often in the responsibility and sustainability literature) is based on the premise that organisations that have a purpose beyond profit, in the form of contributing to environmental sustainability and towards thriving communities, create meaningful work because the purpose of the organisation itself is meaningful. Our research confirms that it is indeed meaningful to people to be able to make a difference within their organisation and towards its major stakeholders. Research participants describe their work as meaningful when they have opportunities to 'give back', 'advocate for the need of others', 'help others to grow', 'replenish the planet', 'help the poor' or 'act with future generations in mind'. Where organisations link their purpose to making a difference, they attract high-quality workers who have pride in their work and workplaces.

At the same time, working towards higher purposes does not, of itself, create meaningful work. Many organisations such as schools, hospitals and NGOs have always worked towards goals of extraordinary consequence, and do attract committed workers because of this. Yet these organisations have far too many unhappy, disengaged or burned-out employees (Maslach and Leiter 1997). Thus, simply changing the purpose of the organisation is not enough to create meaningful work. Unless the dimensions of meaningful work become central to all decision making, employees will still be treated as just another resource in pursuit of a goal, even when the goal is very lofty.

As we have seen in previous chapters, the extent to which work is meaningful is not just dependent on whether individuals can contribute to transcendent goals, although this is one important part of meaningful work. The extent to which work is meaningful depends also on people's ability to:

- speak about what are and are not meaningful tasks, interactions and outcomes in their day-to-day work;

- work in a way that allows them to bring all parts of themselves to work and be alive to every aspect of existence;

- have work in which they are encouraged to act responsibly and constructively towards others as well as themselves;

- combine Doing with Being by also developing sustainability mindsets;

- have work in which they can be inspired and hopeful, but also real and grounded.

Inspiration and Reality

Reality is seen as an opportunity for responsible and sustainable organisations: 'You can view unrealistic expectations as a nuisance to be managed or you can view them as a vaccination against complacency' (Hitchcock and Willard 2006: 8). Corporate Responsibility (CR) can create more ambiguity, where employees are not clear about where the organisation lives up to it's lofty purpose and where it is greenwashing. It is foolish to expect that organisations can live up to their sustainability goals overnight but, without transparency, the gap between Inspiration and Reality cannot be addressed and when this happens, meaningful work diminishes, even in the context of an organisation behaving responsibly. CR is a great opportunity to re-energise the organisation and, at the same time, implementation of CR benefits by consistently facing current reality; companies that have the courage to articulate their core values and to communicate them clearly to insiders and outsiders are inviting the charge of hypocrisy on a regular basis. None of us is immune to observations of disconnection between aspiration and action (Goodpaster 2000: 197).

Being and Doing

Both Integrity with Self and the need for Unity point towards the human need to be, which is naturally aligned with CR. To be responsible, one needs time to *be*. The globalised and technicalised fast pace of organising is itself a key factor that limits the time and space available for the reflection required for ethical decision making (Akrivou *et al.* 2011). While on the one hand people experience a profound opportunity to recreate work, on the other hand they also experience a build-up of pressure and anxiety and 'as the need for reflection grows, the pressures against that need being fulfilled grow too' (Senge *et al.* 2004: 221). People work in an increasingly competitive environment, fraught with mergers, acquisitions, downsizings and subsequent ethical dilemmas. Organisations need members to involve themselves not simply in their given tasks but to reflect on given parameters and seek to change them where necessary. This requires the person to 'be fully there' (Kahn 1992).

Self and Other

Meeting the needs of Self and Other is not just about balancing roles, it is also about a commitment to fulfil the needs of the organisation in a way that is not at the expense of the other person, and future generations. When organisations engage in social and environmental responsibility, employees will increasingly ask whether the product or service truly makes a difference or whether the organisation is just increasing consumption. For example, an employee may question whether the bank they work for sells unnecessary insurance to its elderly customers. At this point the bank may decide that through its employees' acts of volunteering it does enough to placate its most important stakeholders and take no action. However, in doing so it limits its opportunity for CR and is likely to cause disengagement. It has been shown that as ethical awareness strengthens, employees become more concerned about tensions between a firm's economic goals and its duties for social responsibility. When this tension is not addressed it can sap their vitality, lower satisfaction and produce greater levels of job stress (Promislo *et al.* 2012). On the other hand, the bank can decide to ask employees to create services that meet the real needs of elderly customers, in which case it enhances meaningful work as well as CR.

Balancing the different dimensions of meaningful work

The human need to express one's full potential is naturally aligned with CR, which requires the ability to imagine new possibilities and act on them. For example, innovation is required where current ways of production do not meet environmental standards, or useful products cannot be afforded by large parts of the population (Boyd *et al.* 2009). A positive relationship is found between creativity and idealism (Bierly *et al.* 2008), ethics, creativity and moral imagination (Werhane 2007) and ethics, creativity and participation (Collier and Esteban 2007). It is a counterweight to business as usual. So a company that creates opportunities to 'express full potential' not only creates more meaningful work, but is also more likely to meet its responsibilities to society and the environment. At the same time, to sustain both CR and the expressing of full potential, new products, services or practices need to be co-created towards a worthy purpose. When innovation does not connect to the needs of the end-consumers and is done paternalistically 'for' people rather than co-creating it 'with' them, it is neither meaningful nor responsible as it leads to the creation of more stuff rather than responsible production.

An interesting example of this is Oticon, which produced ever more technically sophisticated hearing aids, but when they started to really listen to the customers' needs, found that effectiveness and simplicity were more important than sophistication. They now deliver a very reliable, easy-to-operate, customer-friendly product which balances the needs of the engineers to fully express their creativity and those of the customer, to hear clearly but not be frazzled by too much choice.

Connecting personal meaning and purpose beyond profit

In Chapter 7 we discussed how the Map of Meaning connects individual meaning to organisational purpose. We saw that the Map is useful in creating a strong connection between individual motivation and organisational purpose because it supports building organisational purpose, mission and vision from the bottom up while also building strong relationships within the organisation, a first step to changing the organisation at a profound level.

While the responsibility and sustainability literature clearly recognises how important it is that values are widely shared, far too much guidance on how to create purpose and achieve buy-in is still built on old assumptions about the management of human beings. It still suggests that first the CEO (or a small appointed group) needs to become clear on purpose and values, that they next need to get onto a soapbox and ensure that everyone buys into this purpose, and that this process needs to be tightly controlled because otherwise it becomes unwieldy and fails to lead to action. Yet, as Senge *et al.* point out, this is often counterproductive: 'Sustainability champions . . . frequently end up pushing their ideas into the organization. They achieve marginal impact at best and risk alienating a great many people who might otherwise be open to becoming engaged themselves' (Senge *et al.* 2008: 209). It is also counterproductive because as the champion moves on, the efforts collapse.

When you work with the Map of Meaning, you work from a fundamentally different premise about what it is to be human and this leads to fundamentally different practice: the organisation can only be committed to the extent that individuals within it are committed. We saw earlier how effective it is to use a two-step process when deciding what the organisation stands for (Case study 6.7). Individuals first need to connect to what is meaningful to them before they can connect to, and take responsibility for, the organisational purpose. The advantages of starting with the personal and working out from there to the organisation are described in depth in Chapter 6. That chapter also describes why it is important that all individuals in the organisation, regardless of role or rank, are part of the whole process.

The Map of Meaning offers a structure for moving from what is individually meaningful to statements that are collectively shared. It does so in a manageable way because it allows you to work with what is universal and therefore takes meaningfulness out of the subjective and individualistic to where it is real and jointly owned. At the same time it allows for people to use their own language to express their worldview, connecting the individual in a powerful way to the bigger meanings and principles on which members of the organisation can collectively act, as described in depth in Chapter 3.

A co-created organisational purpose has collective responsibility built into it. Therefore it is more straightforward to generate the practical expression of that purpose because people are already deeply committed to it. They know what needs to happen, and they share a language about this. This leads to immediate and efficient action.

The Map is a simple and constant reminder that legitimises asking questions about how the myriad of decisions made every day by everyone in the organisation affects people's ability to be fully their best. People who are firmly grounded in their own meaning challenge themselves, each other and the organisation to practice what is being preached. This supports ongoing commitment to the purpose of the organisation.

Because the dimensions of meaning are shared, there is more chance for these conversations to be constructive, action-oriented and sometimes even humorous. This can be vital as a balance to the seriousness of organisations with driven purpose.

The Map is also a constant reminder that it is legitimate for the stakeholders of the organisation to ask questions about what the organisation does that helps human flourishing. We discuss this in the next section.

All evidence points towards the need for widely shared ownership of the organisational purpose and the specific values that might flow from it. For example, Rosabeth Moss Kanter (2009) in her study on multinationals found that in companies in which values are widely shared and collectively owned, employees make better decisions, collaborate more effectively and react to opportunity (and crises) more efficiently.

Integrity between actions and systems: working from wholeness

In Chapter 4 we saw how the Map of Meaning enables us to see all elements of meaning together as well as how they relate to each other. We saw how this allows us to experience inner order and integrity. In Chapter 7 we described how fragmentation of organisational practices and disconnection from Self and Others leads to loss of meaning and commitment as people feel pulled in different directions. We showed how the Map is useful in creating not only a sense of shared purpose but also that it helps to create internally integrated systems and practices to support this purpose. Here we show how the Map aids in creating integrity between internal and external organisational values and systems. The need for integrated systems is consistently pointed out in the responsibility and sustainability literature, but nevertheless seems to currently elude many organisations striving for responsible outcomes. As Lynn Sharp Paine (2003: 167) writes:

> Innumerable companies have spawned mini-bureaucracies to administer various special programs—for ethics, diversity, compliance, the environment and so on ... Far too many of these programs are peripheral and largely self-contained activities with

Figure 9.1 **Integrating Sustainability and Meaningful work**

Meaningful Work and Corporate Responsibility

Integration ———————— Fragmentation

Co-creation towards Worthy Purpose

Control towards profit

Dimensions of Meaninful Work:

Stakeholder Commitment	Stakeholder Control
Moral Development	Unity with Others — Compliance
Creating useful things	Integrity with Self — Creating more things
Making a real difference	Expressing Full Potential — Doing enough to placate
Living a full life	Service to Others
	Wholeness — Living a frantic life
Transparency	Inspiration as well as Reality — Ambiguity

Engagement and Corporate Responsibility

Disengagement and diminished Corporate Responsibility

> little connection to the company's main operating systems . . .
> success in meeting the new performance standard will require
> something much more comprehensive and fundamental.

The drive for responsible, sustainable organisations can lead to greater fragmentation and disconnection, and to greater cynicism when it becomes another unfilled promise. 'Far too many people are stifled, constrained, hemmed in, and tied down by bureaucracy and rules that have nothing to do with allowing them to be the best they can be in their jobs' (Carney and Getz 2009: ix). However, the new organisational responsibilities of the organisation provide a unique opportunity to create integrated internal and external systems that are fully integrated and build integrity into every aspect of organising. In Figure 9.1 we map the effects of CR for employees and other stakeholders with and without paying attention to meaningful work.

The human need for unity can be developed to a greater extent when the organisation is in unity with its stakeholder community

When an organisation is already designed around meaningful work, the human need for Unity with Others can naturally expand through corporate social and environmental responsibility, because all members of the organisation already experience how meaningful it is to work together, share values and belong. They solve problems and create opportunities through working together and sharing values with their stakeholders and have a sense of belonging to the wider community. They know the importance of standing up to bullies, including stakeholder bullies. They experience the energy of shared meaning when they work together with customers to create more useful products or services; or when their conversations about values translate into consumer choices. Similarly, work can be infused with meaning through working together with a rich tapestry of stakeholders such as suppliers, communities, NGOs and governments. Thus, in an organisation in which people already experience Unity with Others and are skilful at creating unity, stakeholder engagement naturally aligns with meaningful work and thus draws on the commitment, focus and energy that meaning releases.

Where members of the organisation have not experienced Unity internally, stakeholder engagement can become yet one more independent activity that increases a sense of fragmentation. When people cannot listen to each other in the organisation, nor collaborate, we cannot expect them to have the open, inclusive mindset of world citizenship required by full stakeholder engagement.

The human need to have integrity with self is naturally met in an organisation that is responsive to ethical concerns

Ethics management can become a narrow duty or a tightly controlled activity that increases a sense of fragmentation and depletes employee energy. For example, when members of the organisation have an internal code of ethics that is not a living document they are unlikely to work together on an ongoing basis with external stakeholders to put processes in place that work towards ethical standards. When there are no reflective practices in the organisation to identify deadlines or promotion practices that lead to unethical behaviour internally, it is unlikely that members of the organisation can identify how putting pressure on suppliers to meet tighter deadlines can create unethical behaviour.

Members of the organisation can naturally develop increasing Integrity with Self to a greater extent in an organisation that has high ethical standards. With regard to justice, for example, they will enquire into work conditions throughout the supply chain, asking, what is it that we do that enables others to do the right thing? An organisation that already supports all its members to have Integrity with Self and ask the right questions naturally embraces responsible and sustainable practices, through creating meaningful work.

The human need to express one's full potential is expressed naturally in organisations that explore new opportunities and technologies as well as new ways of thinking and acting

Innovation is very important to responsible organising and to sustainable practice. It is a counterweight to business as usual. Thus an organisation that has already developed a culture and practices that support creativity naturally expands this to create a larger circle of innovation. In *Hybrid Organisations,*

Boyd *et al.* (2009) surveyed companies with purpose beyond profit and found that 83 per cent of these claimed to have had notable innovations relating to product or service. These innovations spanned an enormous range from creating sustainable technology, to finding new ways to source products locally, to co-creating new products with suppliers, to finding innovative ways of serving customers who need the product or service but have not traditionally been able to afford it. Creativity and the sense of achievement that comes from seeing new ideas working is essential in imagining and bringing about a better world, and naturally flows from the creation of meaningful work.

Innovation management can become another independent activity that is disconnected from the human need to create and achieve. If the unique talents of employees have been stifled within the organisation, they are unlikely to see a use for them in activities external to the organisation. If they have had little freedom to look for creative solutions inside the company, they are unlikely to find creative solutions to difficult problems, such as finding new ways of sourcing products locally. When members of the organisation have not been supported to be creative nor experienced a sense of achievement within the organisation, they cannot be expected to arrive at the creative solutions that are required to create a better world. In an organisation that is already designed on the basis of what makes work meaningful, members of the organisation get more opportunities to Express Their Full Potential in relation to the expanding social and environmental responsibilities of the organisation.

The human need for balance is developed naturally in organisations that develop sustainable work practices in which all elements of the map can be expressed

For responsible and sustainable organisations the relationship to time, often expressed in a demand for instant results and tight deadlines, is being rethought at a fundamental level. Responsible organisations by their very nature need to balance long-term effects with immediate results. Several companies now match the pressures of the marketplace with patient capital as a way to get back some control over time. Thus, as the responsible organisation supports meaningful work internally by creating the right balance between Doing and Being through creating relief from goal-directedness and busy-ness, it also learns to create relief from external market pressures and to regularly take time out to reflect on the bigger picture. Moreover, in such organisations it is recognised that people who have meaningful lives outside work not only experience greater well-being and have more energy to bring to work, but are also more likely to ask questions about the responsibility of the organisation towards their families, communities and the environment, as they feel more of a connection to these. Similarly organisations that are already skilful internally at having discussions about the needs of self and others will also be more skilful at addressing the balance between the needs of the organisation itself and that of its stakeholders. For example, we hear of organisations that find it difficult to have conversations about when and how much to give away, for it is hard to determine how much is enough. Yet it is legitimate to ask questions about the right balance between the needs internal to the organisation and those external to it, and such discussions are a natural part of creating meaningful work.

Integrated sustainability practice

There are enormous opportunities for meaningful work in organisations when the internal and external parts of these organisations are connected and operate in ways that complement and extend the interrelatedness of all components. This interconnection is essential to connecting each member of the organisation to its goals. Where this is not in place, even the drive for responsibility and sustainability can lead to greater fragmentation, disorder and loss of integrity, all of which disconnect the members of the organisation from its goals. Fragmentation (and the loss of responsibility and engagement it leads to) cannot be managed by adding more layers of bureaucracy. What is required at this fundamental level of meaning is a conscious awareness of the relationship between patterns internal to the organisation and those external to it and putting systems into place where these can strengthen each other. All the dimensions of meaningful work in the Map of Meaning are therefore not just nice to have, they are essential to responsible and sustainable organising because attending to each of the elements of the Map builds conscious awareness, skills and ongoing commitment to being responsible. At the same time, the responsibility revolution enables each of these meanings to be more fully expressed.

Alternative ways of doing business

In Chapter 3 we discussed how the Map of Meaning helps individuals to have words to articulate what is meaningful to them and how this also enhances collective conversations regarding the bigger questions about what constitutes a life well lived. In Chapter 8 we discussed how this aids people to articulate what is (and is not) of permanent value in these times of rapid organisational change. Here we address how an organisation that is genuinely engaged in corporate responsibility and in taking care of the environment has to make decisions about how best to use its public voice.

A responsible organisation needs to be able to lift its contributions to the public conversation above the economic rationale alone. It needs to speak to who we are as human beings, what makes us well and what makes us happy, to speak beyond purely self-interested conceptualisations of mankind. One of the major contributions of the sustainability movement is that it challenges the view that 'once we have the economy sorted we can attend to other things such as social conditions or the environment'. It is a movement that questions the very foundations and purposes of our lives. Responsible organisations have a responsibility to voice alternative frameworks because these give us choices in conceiving futures in which human beings and the communities in which they live, thrive sustainably.

People cannot thrive when they feel concerned about the future, when too many people around the globe are suffering, when they know that many natural resources such as fish and forests may not be available to their children and when they doubt that our planet will sustain us. In addition, as we have already discussed, people feel very ambivalent about the many ways in which work and the way it is organised, currently affects their lives. Yet as we saw in Chapter 8, it is difficult to speak to alternative frameworks, even when the company aims to become more socially responsible or sustainable. As Lars Kolind, former CEO of Oticon and Grundfos, says:

> With both Oticon and Grundfos, I faced a lot of social and environmental challenges, as well as major issues about our product focus. When I look back upon the decisions that I've lobbied for, they've been on behalf of the environment and social issues—even though if I had been asked at the time what was most important, I probably would have said to make money. As it turns out my focus was and is a very good basis for strategy—and we're making money . . . I can see that I have a much stronger interest in non-financial issues and I am happy that they turned out to make financial sense. I know what I want but I cannot always express why. That can be a problem

> when you deal with the board and all of the financial guys, because
> it is hard for them to accept anything just based on 'knowing it is
> the right decision'. They are so used to focusing on rational
> arguments based on short-term economic results.
>
> Pruzan and Pruzan Mikkelsen 2007: 131

Clearly it is important to speak wisely and with an awareness of the importance of timing when we speak out. But we also need to ask:

- How does the voice of the organisation break free from this limited framework?

- How does it speak consistently across its community of stakeholders, including its shareholders?

- How does the organisation transparently acknowledge who benefits by its existence?

- How does the voice of the organisation encourage democracy, participation and citizenship?

- How does the organisation authentically speak in a way that gives all its members and the world's citizens hope?

We are increasingly hearing business voicing such questions. For instance, Ray Anderson, Founder and Chairman of Interface, asks what the business case is for human extinction,[1] just one example of effectively questioning the status quo.

Trusting the human need for meaning

This whole book is based on the premise that human beings have a need for meaning and that meaning is for them a natural place from which to act. We want to reiterate that this is the case not only in smooth waters but also, and in particular, when they face challenges, be they those of climate change, a desperately needed political or social change or natural disasters.

We have had the chance to see first-hand how people faced with challenges respond by doing what is meaningful. While writing the first edition of this book during the ongoing earthquakes and aftershocks in Christchurch, we observed that people naturally sought meaning. We saw how they, at a point when they were quite literally shaken to the core of their being, brought each of the dimensions of the Map to their actions and sense-making. They did so by serving others, and we often heard people say something like, 'I have to help otherwise I'll go mad'. People from all walks of life – students, farmers, sports, community and religious groups – all came with their shovels and wheelbarrows to clean the streets of silt and sewerage. The (often new immigrant) carers for the elderly walked across a dangerous city to be with their patients. The road-workers toiled day and night and commented when interviewed on radio how great it was to be able to do something and how each pothole they filled made life easier for already distracted drivers. People know that relationships are central to getting through this time. Businesses started working together and, for example, a greengrocer moved in with the coffee shop and a bookshop moved in with the local medical centre. Neighbours met for meals. People spoke to each other on the streets. In the huge catering organisation set up to support all volunteer workers throughout the city, the cooks and cleaners were told to stop work every hour because 'it is important that we get to know each other'.

People expressed their creativity and need for achievement by the creative way they decorated empty spaces where buildings had been demolished and painted the temporary cladding on their houses. They brought skills honed over the years to new heights: for example, men stabilised the cranes so that they continued to work even during the aftershocks.

It was also a time when people went deeply into themselves to find the resources they needed. For example, the builders who, although under great stress, were kind and caring as they dismantled people's homes; the teachers who learned to manage their own fears so that they didn't frighten the children when aftershocks occurred; and all the people who were honest and trustworthy, enabling everyone to more easily share their resources. For example, the priest who said to volunteers, 'You'll find the van with everything you need in it around the front, the keys are in it. Just bring it back when you've finished. And thank you'. And of course they brought it back.

We also heard the numerous voices of ordinary people who, along with professionals in post-disaster planning, recognised what was happening and wrote to the local papers admonishing those in positions of power to recognise these natural ways of being human in the next stage of the planning. Of course, there were those making use of the situation for their own ends, and the chaos and danger of many situations demanded quick and decisive top-down action. Organising and organisations are necessary and at the same time, here as everywhere, the challenge for those rebuilding the city will be to integrate this rich and natural human energy into forms that give it space, and support it to flourish.

Conclusion

The World Health Organization (WHO) has consistently drawn attention to alarming rates of increase in stress and depression. Of course these are not only caused by work, but it has been interesting to note that WHO has been focusing on the relationship between health, well-being and work and has been drawing attention to the fact that stress is not only (or not even primarily) related to the hours we spend at work, or the resources that are available. Being shut out from decision making, dysfunctional workplace relationships and the eroding of time to connect with others all undermine employee well-being and productivity and also increase stress.

It is vital that in the process of creating organisations that are more responsible towards external stakeholders and the environment, we simultaneously take the opportunity to create good work, work that supports people to be their best selves, to make a difference through their work and other parts of their lives, to love and laugh and be their talented and creative selves.

We consistently find that systems that are based on what it is to work meaningfully are, by definition, systems that also promote sustainability. The Map of Meaning provides a simple but very helpful vantage point from which to assess and achieve integration of sustainability practices, and at the same time address employee engagement at a fundamental level.

We need humanity to be capable of more responsible action than it has collectively achieved to date. We believe that by placing the Map of Meaning at the centre of our thinking about organisations we have a reliable map to lead us into the future. It is based on enduring sources of meaning, tested and proven to be relevant in today's world. The Map is grounded at a time when we very much need to keep our feet on the ground. It requires us to face and deal with reality – which is essential – while keeping our connection to the inspiring possibility of what humanity can achieve. It is balanced, when the pressures of the challenges ahead are most likely to tip us into fear and therefore loss of balance, with all the dangers inherent in that. It argues for a unified view of humanity at a time when we most need to practically work with all the people in the world. It supports us in seeing the meaningfulness in each person, to relate to them and ourselves as meaningful and of value, when we most need to respect and value each other. It requires each of us to take equal and full responsibility when it is vital that all people do so. It helps us in knowing ourselves and so helps us attain and retain increasing awareness of ourselves and others. It supports us in being peaceful and mature, and no matter what challenges lie ahead, it calls us to live rich and meaningful lives.

Meaningfulness speaks of the depth of humanity, and it is at this deep level that the potential for a new future lies.

Note

1   www.interfaceglobal.com/getdoc/98a03a4b-65c0–4a61–8984-bc6777b90819/Ray-Watch.aspx, accessed 8 July 2011.

Appendix 1

Joining us in creating more meaningful working lives

Exercise A.1

- What uses for the Map have interested you as you read the book?
- Where might it already be influencing how you think about things?
- Do you have a vision for the ideas in this book?
- How do you see them developing in your life? In your workplace, in your community, in your industry, in your country?
- What role do you see yourself playing in this?
- What support do you need to do this?
- How can we help?
- What would you like to contribute to the wider community of people working with the Map of Meaning?

This book has arisen out of more than twenty years of ongoing work with the Map of Meaning. It has been wonderful work to be involved in, and also challenging. To try to put words to the inner world of meaning, and then to find ways to make this helpful to others, to organisations and society has been a long and confronting task, and ultimately enormously fulfilling.

Where does that leave us as authors? Where does it leave us as a group of committed practitioners? And where does it leave you? What comes next?

In this appendix we discuss our vision for our work, our hopes for the future and how you can become part of this.

We would not have embarked on this work if we did not think that it had the potential to contribute something of great value to our fellow human beings. The further we have progressed with it the more value we have been able to see in it. We hope that has also been your experience in reading this book and in doing the exercises.

The questions in the exercise above are based on the responses that we received from people who read the first edition and have done our workshops. Many have invented new uses for the Map and a number have made it a key aspect of their work. Some of them are the group of supportive practitioners that we have mentioned numerous times in the text. They asked us for this book, and it was largely spurred on by their demand and support that we wrote it. They also talked about wanting a community of practitioners and ways that they could get together with others who use the Map. In response to this we have set up the Map of Meaning International, a charitable trust created to offer information and a connection point for people interested in working with the Map.

Our vision has always been that the Map of Meaning is available in all parts of the world, so that all human beings can access and use it. Since it comes from the wisdom of ordinary people, we simply wish to return it to people. There are a number of ways that we think things might continue from here.

First, use our **website**: www.themapofmeaning.org. On it you will find different areas of interest: using the Map, the services we offer, future development of the Map and work to do with it, plus a list of certified practitioners, lead contacts in different countries, links to talks we have given, academic articles, etc.

Using the Map of Meaning

Copies of the Map

We are happy for you to download copies of the Map and use it. We offer two versions: Appendix 2 lists the names of the key dimensions on it and Appendix 3 contains the outline of the Map; both are useful for the exercises in the book. We request that you use both of these with the copyright attributed to Marjolein Lips-Wiersma.

Brief explanation of the Map

On the website there is a brief explanation of each dimension of the Map, which again we are happy for you to download and use. Again, we request that you leave the wording as it is and the copyright at the bottom.

We will investigate any breach of copyright. This is out of a desire to maintain the academic rigour of the Map and to ensure that the quality of the work remains undiluted.

List of certified practitioners using the Map

As you can see from reading the book, the quality of the work done with the Map is in large measure dependent on the people who facilitate or lead the work. The list covers the countries around the world and the people in them who are certified practitioners with links to their website or contact details. While this list is currently small, we envisage it growing. In the countries where there is no one presently working using the Map you might be inspired to be the person to start. If so, please contact us and we can support you.

Training and certification programme

We are happy to certify people who want to use the Map. To do this you will need to take a course with us that will provide a thorough introduction to the Map and train you to use it effectively. Please contact us if you want to do this training.

Community of practitioners

We have found that the Map really comes alive for people as they begin to use it in their own life and work. So, if you do an Introduction to the Map of Meaning workshop with us, you have the opportunity to join a web-based group that we support for a year. You also have the opportunity to join in any ongoing web-meetings that we run. These meetings, of practitioners from around the world, have proved inspiring and useful and we are delighted to continue to host them.

Services we offer

Our expertise in the Map of Meaning

Please contact us if you would like us, or one of our certified practitioners, to contribute in any of the following ways:

- public speaking;
- facilitating workshops on the Map of Meaning;
- specific interventions and consulting where meaning is important;
- working with policy-makers where meaning is important;
- being part of think-tanks;
- facilitation of topics in which meaning is significant.

Copies of academic papers and articles

These will be uploaded onto our website as we write them.

Blog

We have a blog on our website to keep you up to date with new developments in our work, workshops, writing and any other exciting news.

Future development of the Map of Meaning

New applications of the Map of Meaning

There are many areas where we believe the Map of Meaning has something to offer. Examples of these include:

- curriculum development;
- architecture and meaningful living and meaningful work;
- community development using the Map;
- healing and meaning;

- sustainability and human meaning;

- public policy and human meaning;

- planning meaningful retirement;

- meaning and the Arts;

- parenting using the Map of Meaning;

- meaningful careers;

- meaningful leadership.

However, we do not have the time or resources to do this thinking and development. We are more than happy to support you if you are interested in leading the work. We have done this, for example, in the development of the work on Performance Appraisal about which you read in the book. So please contact us if you would like our input in this way.

Research

We have founded our work on rigorous research and believe it is vitally important that future developments of the Map of Meaning are thoroughly researched. Consequently, we invite Honours, Masters and PhD students to do future research on the Map. So, please contact us if you are interested in this.

An online questionnaire

We are in the process of developing an online questionnaire of the Map of Meaning with the Auckland University of Technology. This will be available through our website.

Forthcoming books

We will provide information about forthcoming books that we are writing, or that others are writing about the Map.

Online courses

We are developing a range of online courses and would be interested to know what topics would be of most interest to you.

In conclusion

Finally, and most of all, we want you to use the Map of Meaning. We have done this work to offer something that is useful to others. It is therefore important to us that these ideas are used by as many people as possible. From the very beginning we have been delighted when workshop participants, leaders, managers and employees immediately began to use the Map in one way or another. We always love hearing about new uses of the Map and are eager to try them out ourselves, so please contact us. We look forward to working with you.

Appendix 2

The Map of Meaning™ with key dimensions

Figure A2.1 **The Map of Meaning**™

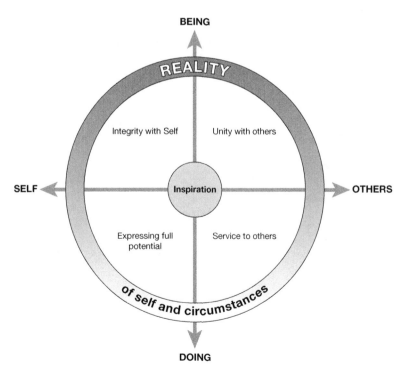

Appendix 3

The Map of Meaning™ blank version

Figure A3.1 **The Map of Meaning**™

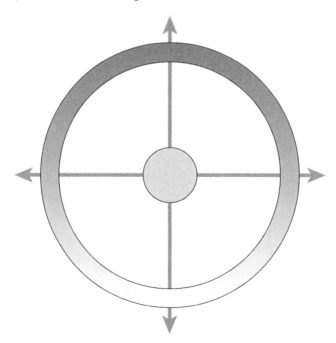

References

Angyal, A. (1965) *Neurosis and Treatment: a Holistic Theory* (New York: Wiley).

Akrivou, K., Bourantas, D., Mo, S. and Papalois, E. (2011). The sound of silence–a space for morality? The role of solitude for ethical decision making. *Journal of Business Ethics* 102(1): 119–33.

Amabile, T. and Kramer, S. (2012). How leaders kill meaning at work. *McKinsey Quarterly* 1: 124–31 [http://tbgleadership.com/wp-content/uploads/2013/04/How-Leaders-Kill-Meaning-At-Work.pdf].

Arendt, H. (2013) *The human condition.* (Chicago, IL: University of Chicago Press).

Ashforth, B.E. and Vaidyanath, D. (2002) Work organizations as secular religions, *Journal of Management Inquiry* 11.4: 359–70.

Bailey, C. and Madden, A. (2015). Time reclaimed: temporality and the experience of meaningful work. *Work, Employment & Society.* Available at http://journals.sagepub.com/doi/pdf/10.1177/0950017015604100

Bailey, C. and Madden, A. (2016). What makes work meaningful – or meaningless. *MIT Sloan Management Review* 57(4).

Bailey, C., Yeoman, R., Madden, A., Thompson, M. and Kerridge, G. (2016). *A Narrative Evidence Synthesis Of Meaningful Work: Progress and a Research Agenda.* Academy of Management Conference, Anaheim, August.

Bakan, D. (1966) *The Duality of Human Existence: Isolation and Communion in Western Man* (Boston, MA: Beacon Press).

Berkelaar, B.L., and Buzzanell, P.M. (2015) Bait and switch or double-edged sword? The (sometimes) failed promises of calling. *Human Relations* 68(1): 157–78.Berry, T. (1988) *The Dream of the Earth* (San Francisco: Sierra Club Books).

Berry, T. (1988) *The Dream of the Earth* (San Francisco: Sierra Club Books).

Bierly, P.E., Kolodinsky, R.W. and Charette, B.J. (2009) Understanding the complex relationship between creativity and ethical ideologies. *Journal of Business Ethics* 86(1): 101–12.

Block, P. (2003) *The Answer to How is Yes: Acting on What Matters Most* (San Francisco: Berrett-Koehler).

—— (2008) *Community: The Structure of Belonging* (San Francisco: Berrett-Koehler).

Blustein, D.L. (2011). A relational theory of working. *Journal of Vocational Behavior* 79(1): 1-17. doi:10.1016/j.jvb.2010.10.004

Boyd, B., Henning, N., Reyna, E., Wang, D.E. and Welch, M.D. (2009) *Hybrid Organizations: New Business Models for Environmental Leadership* (Sheffield, UK: Greenleaf).

Briskin, A. (1998) *The Stirring of Soul in the Workplace* (San Francisco: Berrett-Koehler).

Buber, M. (1970) *I and Thou* (trans. W. Kaufman; New York: Touchstone).

Cameron, K.S. (1986) Effectiveness as paradox: consensus and conflict in conceptions of organizational effectiveness, *Management Science* 32(5): 539–53.

Caproni, P. (1997) Work/life balance, *Journal of Applied Behavioral Science* 1.33: 46–56.

Carney, B.M. and Getz, I. (2009) *Freedom, Inc.: Free Your Employees and Let Them Lead Your Business to Higher Productivity, Profits, and Growth* (New York: Crown Business).

Casey, C. (1999) Come and join our family: discipline and integration in corporate organizational culture, *Human Relations* 52(2): 155–78.

Chalofsky, N.E. (2010) *Meaningful Workplaces: Reframing How and Where We Work* (San Francisco: Jossey-Bass).

Ciulla, J.B. (2000) *The Working Life: The Promise and Betrayal of Modern Work* (New York: Three Rivers).

—— (2004) *Ethics, the Heart of Leadership* (London: Praeger Publishers, 2nd edn).

Collier, J. and Esteban, R. (2007) Corporate social responsibility and employee commitment. *Business Ethics: A European Review* 16(1): 19–33.

Cooperrider, D.L. and Dutton, J.E. (1999) *Organizational Dimensions of Global Change: No Limits to Cooperation* (Thousand Oaks, CA: Sage).

—— and Whitney, D. (2005) *Appreciative Inquiry* (San Francisco: Berrett-Koehler).

Costea, B., Crump, N. and Amiridis, K. (2008) Managerialism, the therapeutic habitus and the self in contemporary organizing, *Human Relations* 61(5): 661–85.

Cottingham, J. (2003) *On the Meaning of Life* (Hove, UK: Psychology Press).

Court, D. (2004) The search for meaning in educational research, *Academic Exchange Quarterly* 8(3): 283–87.

Darley, J.M. and Batson, C.D. (1973) 'From Jerusalem to Jericho': a study of situational and dispositional variables in helping behavior. *Journal of Personality and Social Psychology* 27(1): 100–08. doi:10.1037/h0034449

Dewey, J. (2010) The Mania for Motion, in H. Rosa and W.E. Scheuerman (eds.), *High-speed Society: Social Acceleration, Power and Modernity* (University Park, PA: Pennsylvania State University).

Drucker, P.F. (1994) *The Age of Discontinuity* (New Brunswick, NJ: Transaction).

Ellsworth, R. (2002) *Leading with Purpose: The New Corporate Realities* (Stanford, CA: Stanford University Press).

Evans, P. and Genadry, N. (1999) A duality-based prospective for strategic human resource management, research and theory, in J.B. Shaw, P.S. Kirkbride, L.D. Dyer and J. Boudreau (eds), *Strategic Human Resources Management: An Agenda for the 21st Century* (Stamford, CT: JAI).

Frankl, V. (1963) *Man's Search for Meaning: An Introduction to Logotherapy* (New York: Washington Square).

Fritz, H. L. and Helgeson, V. S. (1998). Distinctions of unmitigated communion from communion: self-neglect and overinvolvement with others. *Journal of Personality and Social Psychology* 75(1): 121.

Goodpaster, K.E. (2000) Conscience and its counterfeits in organizational life: A new interpretation of the naturalistic fallacy, *Business Ethics Quarterly* 10(1): 189–201.

—— (2007) *Conscience and Corporate Culture* (Malden, MA: Blackwell).

Grant, A.M. (2007). Relational job design and the motivation to make a prosocial difference. *Academy of Management Review* 32, 393–417.

Gruen, A. (1999) *Heaven Begins Within You: Wisdom from the Desert Fathers* (New York: Crossroad).

Hampden-Turner, C.M. (1990) *Corporate Culture: From Vicious to Virtuous Circles* (London: Hutchinson/Economist).

Handy, C. (1994) *The Age of Paradox* (Boston, MA: Harvard Business School Press).

Havel, V. (2004) An orientation of the heart, in P.R. Loeb (ed.), *The Impossible Will Take a Little While: A Citizen's Guide to Hope in a Time of Fear* (New York: Basic).

Hermans, H.J.M. and Hermans, E. (1995) *Self-Narratives: The Construction of Meaning in Psychotherapy* (New York: Guilford).

Herzog, W. and Cronin, P. (2002) *Herzog on Herzog* (London: Faber & Faber).

Hitchcock, D. and Willard, M. (2006) *The Business Guide to Sustainability: Practical Strategies and Tools for Organizations* (London: Earthscan).

Hollender, J. and Breen, B. (2010) *The Responsibility Revolution: How the Next Generation of Business Will Win* (San Francisco: Jossey-Bass).

hooks, b. (2009) *Belonging: A Culture of Place* (New York, NY: Routledge).

Howard, S. and Welbourn, D. (2004) *The Spirit at Work Phenomenon* (London: Azure).

Humle, D.M. (2014) The ambiguity of work. *Nordic Journal of Working Life Studies*, March.

Jackall, R. (1988) *Moral Mazes: The World of Corporate Managers* (San Francisco: Jossey-Bass).

Jackson, I. and Nelson, J. (2004) *Profits with Principles* (New York: Doubleday).

Jordan, S., Messner, M., and Becker, A. (2009) Reflection and mindfulness in organizations: Rationales and possibilities for integration. *Management Learning* 40(4): 465–73.

Kahn, W.A. (1992) To be fully there: psychological presence at work. *Human Relations* 45(4): 321–49.

——. (2001) Holding Environments at Work. *The Journal of Applied Behavioral Science* 37(3): 260–79.

Kahn, W. A. and Fellows, S. (2013). Employee engagement and meaningful work, in Byrne, Z., Dik, B. and Steger, M. (eds), *Purpose and Meaning in the Workplace* (Chapter 5) (Washington, DC: American Psychological Association).

Kanter, R.M. (2009) *Supercorp: How Vanguard Companies Create Innovation, Profit and Growth* (New York: Crown Business).

Klein, L. (2008) *The Meaning of Work: Papers on Work Organization and the Design of Jobs* (London: Karnac).

Kofodimos, J. (1993) *Balancing act, how managers can integrate successful careers and fulfilling personal lives.* (San Francisco, CA: Jossey-Bass).

Korosec, K. (2010) Why You're Doing Performance Reviews All Wrong [www.brittenassociates.com/articles.htm, accessed 6 July 2011].

Krishnamurti, J. (1973) *The Awakening of Intelligence* (London: Victor Gollancz).

Lindström, S. (2016). 'An army of our own': legitimating the professional position of HR through well-being at work. *Scandinavian Journal of Management* 32(4): 189–96. doi:10.1016/j.scaman.2016.08.003

Lips-Wiersma, M.S. (1999) The influence of 'spiritual meaning-making' on career choice, transition and experience (Doctoral dissertation, University of Auckland).

—— (2000) The Spiritual Meaning of Work (PhD thesis, University of Auckland).

—— (2002) Analysing the career concerns of spiritually oriented people: lessons for contemporary organizations, *Career Development International* 7(7): 385–97.

Lips-Wiersma, M. (2006) The role of spiritual retreats in higher education: the necessity for, and difficulties with, reflection on lasting values in a new public management context. *Public Administration and Development* 26: 123–33.

—— and Mills, C. (2002) Coming out of the closet: negotiating spiritual expression in the workplace, *Journal of Managerial Psychology* 17(3): 183–202.

—— and Morris, L. (2009) Discriminating between 'meaningful work' and the 'management of meaning', *Journal of Business Ethics* 88(3): 491–511.

—— (2011) *The map of meaning: A guide to sustaining our humanity in the world of work.* (Yorkshire, UK: Greenleaf Publishing).

—— and Wright, S. (2012) Measuring the meaning of meaningful work: Development and validation of the Comprehensive Meaningful Work Scale (CMWS). *Group and Organization Management* 37(5): 655–85.

Lips-Wiersma, M., Soutter, A. and Wright, S. (2015) The lived experience of meaningful work. *New Zealand Journal of Human Resources Management* 15: 134–50.

Lips-Wiersma, M, Wright, S. and Dik, B. (2016) Meaningful work: differences among blue-, pink- and white-collar occupations. *Career Development International* 21(5): 534–51.

Littleton, S., Arthur, M.B. and Rousseau, D. (2000) The future of boundaryless careers, in A. Collin & R. Young (eds), *The Future of Careers.* (Cambridge, UK: Cambridge University Press).

Llorens, S., Schaufeli, W., Bakker, A. and Salanova, M. (2007) Does a positive gain spiral of resources, efficacy beliefs and enagement exist? *Computers and Human Behavior* 23: 825–41.

Marshall, J. (1989) Re-visioning career concepts: a feminist invitation, in M.B. Arthur, D.T. Hall and B.S. Lawrence (eds.), *A Handbook of Career Theory* (Cambridge, UK: Cambridge University Press): 275–91.

Maslach, C. and Leiter, M.P. (1997) *The Truth about Burnout: How Organizations Cause Personal Stress and What to do About It* (San Francisco: Jossey-Bass).

McAdams, D.P. (1992) Unity and purpose in human lives: the emergence of identity as a life story, in R.A. Zucker, A.I. Rabin, J. Aronoff and S. Frank (eds.), *Personality Structure in the Life Course: Essays on Personality in the Murray Tradition* (New York: Springer): 323–75.

McKenzie, J. (1996) *Paradox, the Next Strategic Dimension: Using Conflict to Re-energize Your Business* (London: McGraw-Hill).

Mitroff, I.I. and Linstone, H. (1993) *The Unbound Mind: Breaking the Chains of Traditional Business Thinking* (Oxford: Oxford University Press).

Morin, E.M. (1995) Organizational effectiveness and the meaning of work, in T. Pauchant (ed.), *In Search of Meaning: Managing for the Health of Our Organizations, Our Communities, and the Natural World* (San Francisco: Jossey-Bass): 29–64.

Nicoll, M. (1957) *Psychological Commentaries on the Teaching of G.I. Gurdjieff and P.D. Ouspensky* (London: Vincent Stuart).

Noonan, J. (2009) Free time as a necessary condition of free life. *Contemporary Political Theory* 8(4): 377–93. doi: http://dx.doi.org/10.1057/cpt.2008.27

O'Donohue, J. (1998) *Anam Cara: A Book of Celtic Wisdom* (New York: Harper Perennial).

—— (2000) *Eternal Echoes: Exploring our Hunger to Belong* (London Bantam).

O'Reilley, M.R. (1998) *Radical Presence: Teaching as Contemplative Practice* (Portsmouth, NH: Heinemann).

Overell, S. (2009) *Inwardness: The Rise of Meaningful Work* (Provocation Series 4.2.; London: The Work Foundation).

Paine, L. S. (2003) *Value Shift: Why Companies Must Merge Social and Financial Imperatives to Achieve Superior Performance* (New York: McGraw-Hill).

Palmer, P. (1990) *The Active Life: A Spirituality of Work, Creativity and Caring* (San Francisco: Jossey-Bass).

—— (2004) *A Hidden Wholeness: The Journey toward an Undivided Life* (San Francisco: Jossey-Bass).

Parkins, W. (2004) Out of time: fast subjects and slow living. *Time & Society* 13: 363–82.

Parry, K.W. and Bryman, A. (2006) Leadership in organizations, in S.R. Clegg, C. Hardy, T.B. Lawrence and W.R. Nord (eds.), *The Sage Handbook of Organization Studies* (London: Sage, 2nd edn): 447–68.

Pauchant, T.C. (ed.) (1995). *In Search of Meaning: Managing for the Health of Our Organizations, Our Communities, and the Natural World* (San Francisco: Jossey-Bass).

Pavlish, C. and Hunt, R. (2012) An exploratory study about meaningful work in acute care nursing. *Nursing Forum* 47(2): 113–22. doi:10.1111/j.1744-6198.2012.00261.x

Pozzi, D. and Williams, S. (1998) *Success with Soul: New Insights to Achieving Success with Real Meaning* (Melbourne, VIC: Dorian Welles Proprietary).

Pratt, M. G., Pradies, C. and Lepisto, D. A. (2013) Doing well, doing good, and doing with: organizational practices for effectively cultivating meaningful work, in Byrne, Z., Dik, B. and Steger, M. (eds), *Purpose and Meaning in the Workplace* (Washington, DC: American Psychological Association): 173–93.

Promislo, M.D., Giacalone, R.A. and Welch, J. (2012). Consequences of concern: ethics, social responsibility and well-being. *Business Ethics: A European Review* 21(2): 209–19.

Pruzan, P. and Pruzan Mikkelsen, K. (2007) *Leading with Wisdom: Spiritual-based Leadership in Business* (Sheffield, UK: Greenleaf).

Qin, X., DiRenzo, M.S., Xu, M. and Duan, Y. (2014) When do emotionally exhausted employees speak up? Exploring the potential curvilinear relationship between emotional exhaustion and voice. *Journal of Organizational Behavior* 35(7): 1018–41.

Quinn, R.E. (1988) *Beyond Rational Management: Mastering the Paradoxes and Competing Demands of High Performance* (San Francisco: Jossey-Bass).

Ready, D. and Conger, J. (2008) Enabling bold visions. *MIT Sloan Management Review*, 1 January.

Ritzenberg, A. (2012). *The Sentimental Touch: The Language of Feeling in the Age of Managerialism* (Oxford: Oxford University Press).

Robinson, J.P., Godbey, G. and Putnam, R.D. (1999) *Time for Life: The Surprising Ways Americans Use Their Time* (University Park, PA: Pennsylvania State University Press).

Rosa, H. (2013) *Social Acceleration: A New Theory of Modernity* (New York: Colombia University Press).

Rosso, B., Dekas, K. and Wrzesniewski, A. (2010) On the meaning of work: a theoretical integration and review, *Research in Organizational Behavior* 30: 91–127.

Scharmer, O. (2007) *Theory U: Leading from the Future as it Emerges* (San Francisco: Berrett-Koehler).

Scheuerman, W.E. (2010) Citizenship and Speed, in H. Rosa and W.E. Scheuerman (eds), *High-Speed Society: Social Acceleration, Power and Modernity* (University Park, PA: Pennsylvania State University): 287–306.

Schumacher, E.F. (1978) *A Guide for the Perplexed* (London: Sphere).

Schwartz, B. and Sharpe, K.E. (2006) Practical wisdom: Aristotle meets positive psychology. *Journal of Happiness Studies* 7(3): 377–95.

Schwartz, H.S. (1995) Acknowledging the dark side of organizational life, in T.C. Pauchant (ed.), *In Search of Meaning: Managing for the Health of Our Organizations, Our Communities, and the Natural World* (San Francisco: Jossey-Bass): 224–43.

Senge, P. (1997) *The Fifth Discipline* (London: Century).

—— (2010) *The Necessary Revolution: Working Together to Create a Sustainable World* (New York: Broadway Books).

——, Scharmer, O., Jaworksi, J. and Flowers, B. (2004) *Presence: Human Purpose and the Field of the Future* (Cambridge, MA: Society for Organizational Learning).

Senge, P. *et al.* (2008). *The Necessary Revolution: Working Together to Create a Sustainable World* (London: Crown Business).

Sennett, R. (2006) *The Culture of New Capitalism* (New Haven, CT: Yale University Press).

Sievers, B. (1994) *Work, Death and Life Itself: Essays on Management and Organization* (Berlin: Walter de Gruyter).

Sinek, S. (2009). *Start With Why: How Great Leaders Inspire Everyone to Take Action* (London: Penguin).

Skolimowski, H. (1994) *The Participatory Mind* (London: Arkana).

Sykes, K. (2007) The quality of public dialogue. *Science* 318(5855): 1349.

Tams, S. and Marshall, J. (2011) Responsible careers: systemic reflexivity in shifting landscapes. *Human Relations* 64(1): 109–31. doi:10.1177/0018726710384292

Tippet, K. (2016) *Becoming Wise: An Inquiry into the Mystery and Art of Living* (London: Penguin).

Vaill, P.B. (1996) *Learning as a Way of Being: Strategies for Survival in a World of Permanent White Water* (San Francisco: Jossey-Bass).

Vince, R. (2002) Organizing Reflection. *Management Learning* 33(1): 63–78.

Von Bergen, C., Campbell, K. and Leird, R. (2016) Too much of a good thing in employment counseling. *Academy of Educational Leadership Journal* 20(1): 143.

Vostal, F. (2015) Academic life in the fast lane: The experience of time and speed in British academia. *Time & Society* 24(1): 71–95.

Werhane, P.H. (2007). Corporate social responsibility/corporate moral responsibility. *The Debate over Corporate Social Responsibility* 459.

Wheatley, M. (2002) *Turning to One Another: Simple Conversations to Restore Hope to the Future* (San Francisco: Berrett-Koehler).

Williamson, M. (1992) *A Return to Love: Reflections on the Principles of a Course in Miracles* (New York: HarperCollins).

Willmott, H. (1993) Strength is ignorance; slavery is freedom: managing culture in modern organizations. *Journal of Management Studies* 40(4): 515–52.

Wrzesniewski, A. and Dutton, J. E. (2001) Crafting a job: revisioning employees as active crafters of their work. *Academy of Management Review 26*(2): 179–201.

Yalom, I.D. (1980) *Existential Psychotherapy* (New York: Basic Books).

About the authors

Marjolein Lips-Wiersma is Professor of Ethics and Sustainability Leadership at the Auckland Institute of Technology, New Zealand. Over the past twenty years she has done research on meaningful work. She has been a board director, chair of the Management, Spirituality and Religion group of the Academy of Management, and regularly works with individuals, groups and organisations to create meaningful work practices. Her academic work has won several awards and has been published in top journals. She has integrated the theme of meaningful work into a wide range of teaching including undergraduate business ethics, postgraduate responsible leadership and executive MBA organisational behaviour. Marjolein is a Founding Director of the Map of Meaning International.

Lani Morris has over 30 years' experience of working as an independent organisational behaviour practitioner with organisations and individuals in New Zealand, Australia and the United Kingdom and as a contract lecturer at a number of universities and tertiary institutions. She has a BA in the humanities, and an MBA and an MSc in Responsibility and Business Practice from the University of Bath. She has studied the human search for meaning all her life, through philosophy and comparative religion in her undergraduate degree and through independent study since then. The key focus of her work is to help people take responsibility for and reclaim power over themselves, their lives and their work. Her expertise includes: leadership, motivation, clear communication, creativity and meaningful work. She has worked with the Map of Meaning since 2000. Lani is a Founding Director of the Map of Meaning International.

Index

Printed in Great Britain
by Amazon